Contents

Page

Chapter 1
Introduction

1-1. Purpose

a. TRADOC Pam 525-2-1 describes how future Army forces will conduct intelligence operations in support of full-spectrum operations. It articulates in practical terms the abstract ideas presented in the ACC and AOC, conceptualizes the operational and tactical employment of intelligence units, guides future force development, and identifies the capabilities needed to succeed at the operational and tactical levels. The ideas introduced in the ACC and AOC are central to the way the Army will fight and win. The role of U.S. Army intelligence within the conditions described in the ACC and AOC concepts is to mitigate uncertainty and support commanders' situational awareness in support of full-spectrum operations. Army intelligence will accomplish these missions by providing organic intelligence capabilities at each echelon and reinforce those capabilities as required from Generating Force and other nondeployed resources while integrating all sources of information.

b. TRADOC Pam 525-2-1 provides the conceptual basis for development of the following core intelligence disciplines: All-source intelligence, counterintelligence (CI), human intelligence (HUMINT), geospatial intelligence (GEOINT), measurement and signature intelligence (MASINT), open source intelligence (OSINT), signals intelligence (SIGINT), and technical intelligence (TECHINT). For purposes of this concept, police intelligence (resident at the Maneuver Support Center of Excellence) is also addressed. Collectively, this suite of multidisciplined intelligence capabilities along with synchronization of intelligence, surveillance, and reconnaissance establishes the foundation, across doctrine, organization, training, materiel, leadership and education, personnel and facilities (DOTMLPF), for intelligence support to the Army's vision of how it will fight and operate in the future amid conditions of uncertainty in complex environments.

c. These core disciplines and intelligence, surveillance, and reconnaissance synchronization are integral to six driving capabilities. These are: full motion video; SIGINT (geo-location); HUMINT (interrogations); document and media exploitation; HUMINT (source operations); and SIGINT (internals).

d. These six driving capabilities are enabled by intelligence, surveillance, and reconnaissance architecture and dissemination; analysis and exploitation; and communications.

1-2. Background

a. The operational environment of 2010 looks far different from what the Army envisioned at the start of this century. Protracted conflicts in both Afghanistan and Iraq proved the fallacy of concepts based on near-perfect intelligence, assured transport layers, lines of communication, and over-reliance on precision guided munitions. Recent and ongoing conflicts highlighted the limitations of technology and the paramount importance of the human dimensions of war. Wars in Georgia, Lebanon, and Gaza confirmed trends observed in Afghanistan and Iraq. The Army must reinforce the timeless principles of war and enduring ideas of earlier concepts while applying lessons learned over the last 9 years. Since the start of Operation Enduring Freedom (OEF) and Operation Iraqi Freedom (OIF), Army intelligence has made a massive and concerted effort to reinvigorate tactical echelon HUMINT capabilities. By investing in significant force structure changes, HUMINT capabilities that had atrophied after the Cold War and the subsequent collapse of the former Soviet Union are now firmly in place and a significant contributor to the successful prosecution of "war among the people." The January 2010 paper, *Fixing Intel, A Blueprint for making Intelligence Relevant in Afghanistan,*[1] served to broaden the discussion about what intelligence activities should be doing in support of their commanders, and expanded the traditional focus of intelligence collection and analytical efforts beyond the usual emphasis on "red" activities. The projected future operating environment stresses that these types of activities will remain a constant for the foreseeable future. Additionally, threats of spill over violence along shared U.S. borders require the discovery of potential threats before they reach the U.S.

b.   Intelligence improvement strategies historically addressed the changing operational environment by creating sensors and analytical systems designed to locate hierarchical centrally-directed combat formations and predict their actions in high-intensity conflict. These strategies assumed that intelligence forces, if properly refocused, would remain sufficiently relevant and effective during stability operations and irregular warfare and not require major programmatic or structural changes for these missions. Both the current operational environment and the future operational environment describe decentralized threat networks, network-of-networks, or even networks enabled to act as surrogates for nation-states. These networks necessitate resolution at the identity level, temporal resolution (minutes or less), and geolocation resolution at the house and/or vehicle level (or lower). The ongoing military intelligence rebalance efforts were created to recommend solutions to the intelligence force structure that optimizes intelligence support to Army full-spectrum operations.

c.   In December 2009, the Army published the ACC followed in August 2010 by the AOC. These documents describe the broad capabilities the Army and Army intelligence will require to overcome a combination of adaptive threats and adaptive adversaries in complex operating environments. Within the Army concept framework, the ACC and AOC provide the conceptual foundation and background for TRADOC Pam 525-2-1 and follow-on capability based assessments needed to develop new Army intelligence capabilities.

d.   To operate effectively under conditions of uncertainty and complexity in an era of persistent conflict, future forces and leaders must strive to mitigate uncertainty through understanding the situation in depth, developing the situation through action, fighting for information, and reassessing the situation to keep pace with the dynamic nature of conflict. Future intelligence forces gain and maintain contact with the enemy; collect signatures and observables to identify, locate, and provide intentions of threat forces and threat networks to facilitate a greater understanding of the terrain and civil considerations within an area of operations. Further, intelligence must anticipate the spillover of violence and threats of spillover of violence along shared borders requiring the discovery of potential threats before they reach the U.S. homeland.   However, commanders must still make decisions based on incomplete, inaccurate, or contradictory information. Accomplishing challenging intelligence missions and responding to a broad range of adaptive threats under conditions of uncertainty will require multifunctional Army intelligence capabilities that exhibit a high degree of *operational adaptability and flexibility.* The future force must be able to conduct effective intelligence collection, analysis, and dissemination in support of combined arms operations in the area of operations (AO). Building on the foundation of existing intelligence capabilities and capacity, Army intelligence must hone its ability to gain, sustain, and exploit those capabilities and capacity to support future Army forces combined arms operations. The central idea, supporting ideas, and core operational actions of the ACC, AOC, and the components of the solution of TRADOC PAM 525-2-1 promote such a mindset and provide the conceptual foundation for an Army intelligence force that can support the commander in full-spectrum operations.

e. TRADOC Pam 525-2-1 describes the operational environment, how Army intelligence forces will conduct collection and analysis by applying the lessons learned during the last 9 years of conflict, and discussing requirements Army intelligence may need across DOTMLPF to field a force able to meet future challenges. TRADOC Pam 525-2-1 consists of four chapters. Chapter 1 introduces the Army concept framework and Army operational concept which provides the assumptions that guide TRADOC Pam 525-2-1. Chapter 2 presents the Army intelligence problem, central idea, and solution, along with a number of supporting ideas. Chapter 3 discusses intelligence support to ACC core operational actions, and chapter 4 provides the pamphlet's conclusion.

1-3. The operational environment

a. The operational environment (OE) summary below, drawn from the *TRADOC Operational Environment, 2009-2025,* is intended to set the stage for the sections that follow by providing context for discussing TRADOC Pam 525-2-1 and the resulting required capabilities. The future OE will present the Army with complex and challenging conditions. It will remain difficult to predict and is subject to radical changes and singularities. It may encompass hybrid threats that create multiple dilemmas for our maneuver forces by simultaneous employment of regular and irregular forces, and criminal elements, using an ever-changing variety of conventional and unconventional tactics. Future adversaries will possess weapons of mass destruction (WMD) and technology allowing them to be disruptive over widespread areas.

b. Future adversaries are expected to attack U.S. operational patterns and predictability; take advantage of U.S. operational constraints; avoid perceived U.S. strengths; and exploit perceived lack of cultural understanding.

c. Adversaries will seek conventional and irregular capabilities; employ a range of technologies; utilize information warfare as a key weapon system; and employ complex battle positions.

d. Just as U.S. forces have learned and adapted, adversaries have as well. Their lessons learned include the following:

(1) High-tech weapons and communications systems can be countered with low-tech responses and high-tech threat capabilities.

(2) The U.S. military is slow to react to information operations (IO) so adversaries will seek to control the message and the fight.

(3) Army maneuver forces are often predictable in their operations.

(4) U.S. operations can be derailed over time through a strategy of exhaustion.

(5) U.S. forces distributed over wide areas can be successfully attacked and casualties inflicted which may impact U.S. resolve.

(6) Antiaccess, access denial, and tactical shielding are effective means of influencing U.S. response and controlling the ability of U.S. forces to react in theater.

e. What does this future operational environment mean for U.S. adversaries?

(1) Adversaries are not required to counter U.S. military power symmetrically; instead, they will employ a combination of unconventional, irregular, and blended forces. The enemy will use the total war construct, achieving success by attacking across all the dimensions of power—political, military, economic, social, infrastructure, information physical environment, and time (PMESII-PT).

(2) Adversaries will blend in with the environment and attack the U.S. communication architecture, intelligence gathering systems, and sustainment lines of communication. They will target U.S. reliance on contractors and private security forces to create unfavorable conditions and discourage further contract support.

(3) Adversaries will attempt to exploit U.S. forces' lack of cultural understanding to alienate the local populace.

(4) Adversaries will create alliances between nations and including nonstate actors that support access denial that will hinder U.S. staging efforts and will force U.S. forces to seek alternative, less desirable, and time consuming methods of entry.

(5) Adversaries will conduct tactical actions directed towards achieving information warfare objectives rather than purely military ones. Information, communications, and technology will continue to proliferate. A wide variety of actors with access to and operating outside the control of the military will be part of any future OE. Information cyber attacks can cause widespread disruption.

f. What does this future operational environment mean for U.S. Army leaders?

(1) Army leaders will need to embrace the concept of complexity and understand that they will operate and function with some level of uncertainty.

(2) Army leaders will often operate over wide areas.

(3) Army leaders will operate under near continuous media scrutiny, potentially giving local events global significance.

(4) To achieve speed of action, identify and exploit opportunities, and protect against unanticipated dangers, Army leaders apply an expanded concept of combined arms and operate decentralized consistent with the tenets of mission command.

(5) Army leaders must be operationally adaptable.

(6) Army leaders must be prepared to operate in environments where WMD are likely to be used.

g.   For the foreseeable future, Army intelligence Soldiers, leaders, and units will remain globally engaged – called on to execute missions across the spectrum of conflict.

1-4. The intelligence warfighting function

a.   The intelligence warfighting function is the related tasks and systems that facilitate understanding of the operational environment, enemy, terrain, and civil consideration.[2]   It includes tasks associated with intelligence, surveillance, and reconnaissance operations and is driven by the commander. Intelligence is more than just collection. It is a continuous process that involves analyzing information from all sources and conducting operations to develop the situation.

b.   Intelligence is not passive; it is an active foundational function of the Army. Intelligence operations are the variety of intelligence and counterintelligence tasks that are carried out by various intelligence organizations and activities within the intelligence process. Intelligence operations include planning and direction, collection, processing and exploitation, analysis and production, dissemination and integration, and evaluation and feedback. Intelligence operations gain and maintain contact with threat forces; collect signatures and observables to identify, locate, and provide intentions of threat forces and threat networks. Intelligence operations are not solely accomplished from airborne platforms or standoff surveillance sites. They are often executed in and amongst local populations and in close proximity to threat forces and/or groups. Intelligence operations also facilitate understanding of the terrain and civil considerations within an area of operations.

c.   Intelligence operations are conducted to provide intelligence in support of all missions. The primary focus of Army intelligence operations is generating tactical intelligence such as, intelligence that supports the planning and conduct of operations. Although the focus is on tactical intelligence, the Army draws on both strategic and operational intelligence resources and, in certain circumstances, conducts intelligence operations at the operational and even strategic level.

d.   The intelligence warfighting function is a flexible force of personnel, organizations, and equipment that, individually or collectively, provide commanders with the timely, relevant, accurate, predictive, and tailored intelligence required to visualize the AO, assess the situation, and direct military actions. Additionally, the intelligence warfighting function is a complex system that operates worldwide, from below ground to space, in support of an operation, to include the ability to leverage theater and national capabilities. It requires cooperation and division of intelligence, surveillance, and reconnaissance and analysis efforts internally, higher, lower, adjacent, and across components and multinational forces.

e. Planning and executing military operations will require intelligence regarding the threat (traditional, irregular, catastrophic, and disruptive), civil considerations, and the AO. The intelligence warfighting function generates intelligence and intelligence products that portray the enemy and aspects of the environment. These intelligence products enable the commander to identify potential courses of action, plan operations, employ forces effectively, employ effective tactics and techniques, and implement protection.

f. The intelligence warfighting function is always engaged in offensive, defensive, stability, and when directed, civil support operations. Intelligence supports decisionmaking. Hard training, thorough planning, meticulous preparation, and aggressive execution posture the Army for success. In the current and future environment, the Army must maintain intelligence readiness to support operations. This support reaches across full-spectrum operations and levels of war to produce the intelligence required to accomplish the mission successfully through a combination of space, aerial, seaborne, and ground-based systems to provide the most comprehensive intelligence possible. During force projection operations, the intelligence warfighting function supports the commander with accurate and responsive intelligence from predeployment through redeployment.

g. Within the framework of the intelligence warfighting function, the intelligence tasks and the intelligence process, intelligence personnel further focus on conducting intelligence from a fundamental enterprise perspective. The Army intelligence enterprise is the sum total of the networked and federated systems, and efforts of the military intelligence personnel (to include collectors and analysts), sensors, organizations, information, and processes that allow the focus necessary to use the power of the entire intelligence community (IC). The purpose of the Army intelligence enterprise is to provide technical support and guidance as well as an information and intelligence architecture that efficiently and effectively synchronize intelligence, surveillance, and reconnaissance operations and intelligence analysis and production to drive intelligence production in support of the commander's situational awareness and understanding.

1-5. Assumptions

a. These intelligence assumptions connect the ACC to AOC to TRADOC Pam 525-2-1 (strategic, operational, and tactical context). The following assumptions for 2016-2028 require a reassessment of the functional intelligence concept through experimentation, verification, and validation. The assumptions are organized into three focus areas: operational environment, organizational, and technological.

b. Operational environment.

(1) National, joint, and Army intelligence collection will be conducted in complex and urban terrain.

(2) The enemy will use the "span of technology" ranging from tactical radios to fiber optics and beyond to frustrate U.S. collection and exploitation efforts.

(3) The U.S. will maintain the capability to employ collection and analysis assets (ground, air, cyberspace, and maritime) in any theater against all intelligence discipline targets.

(4) Required Army policies (authorizations and restrictions) will be specified for intelligence operations in support of homeland security.

c. Organizational. The human resources required are available and are trained, technically well informed, and culturally astute and language qualified across the intelligence disciplines.

d. Technological.

(1) The technological base is sustained and adequate research and development funding is available. Long-term focus is sustained for each intelligence discipline in the key areas of computing hardware, communication, and software development.

(2) The Army is cognizant of and can match the rate of technological change largely driven by the commercial sector.

(3) The Army extends the lives of existing technical sensors by developing better processing capabilities to discover and exploit data that we did not know was present.

(4) The Army initiates a concerted effort to develop new and enable existing technical sensors to strip away the concealment provided to our enemies by the urban and complex terrain environment.

e. To develop TRADOC Pam 525-2-1, subject matter experts in all intelligence disciplines from the Intelligence Center of Excellence and TRADOC developed and staffed drafts of this concept. The writers examined eight types of operations to set the context for discussion of organizational and functional roles, challenges, and interdependencies. The writers also considered how the Army would execute the core operational actions in the context of specific scenarios and what commensurate intelligence support would be required. The sections that follow include the linkage to the ACC and AOC.

1-6. Linkage to the Army capstone concept

a. The ACC identifies six supporting ideas that contribute to the future forces' ability to apply operational adaptability in future operations. They are develop the situation through action; conduct combined arms operations; employ a combination of defeat and stability mechanisms; integrate joint capabilities; cooperate with partners; and exert psychological and technical influence.

b. The ACC also identifies a set of core operational actions to meet future security challenges. The core operational actions range from engagement of allies and indigenous forces, such as security force assistance and the conduct of full-spectrum operations, to defeat the enemy and ensure progress toward achieving strategic objectives.

c. TRADOC Pam 525-2-1 is linked to the ACC by acknowledging the need for intelligence to develop operational adaptability and to broaden analysis beyond military-focused intelligence preparation of the battlefield to intelligence preparation of the OE.

1-7. Linkage to the AOC

a. The AOC links to a future force set of ACC core operational actions to meet future security challenges (see figure 1-1). The seven core operational actions of the ACC address broadly the nature and type of operations the Army will conduct as part of a joint force. The core operational actions provide the common conceptual threads of continuity between the ACC, the AOC, and TRADOC Pam 525-2-1.

Core Operational Actions
Conduct security force assistance
Shaping and entry operations
Intertheater and intratheater operational maneuver
Full-spectrum operations
Conduct overlapping protection operations
Distributed support and sustainment
Network-enabled mission command

Figure 1-1. Core operational actions

b. The AOC further specifies six supporting ideas that contribute to the Army's ability to conduct combined arms maneuver and security operations: conduct decentralized operations, integrate intelligence and operations, conduct air-ground operations, expand capabilities at brigade level, inform and influence populations, conduct effective transitions, and enhance unit cohesion.

c. TRADOC Pam 525-2-1 is linked to the AOC by acknowledging the need to improve operations intelligence interface; provide flexible organizational designs; improve capability to operate in complex and urban terrain; enhance critical thinking skills; strengthen integration with joint and interagency partners; develop better collectors and/or sensors tied to signatures of interest; and development better and more efficient use and analysis of data.

1-8. Linkage to the human dimension
The human dimension emphasizes optimization of the cognitive, physical, and social components of every Soldier with the objective to improve the acquisition and selection of personnel; maximize leader and organizational development; establish the ability to rapidly adjust, deliver, and provide accessibility of training and education ultimately balancing Soldier knowledge, skills, and abilities with full-spectrum operation mission requirements.

1-9. References

Required and related publications are in appendix A.

1-10. Explanations of abbreviations and terms

Abbreviations and special terms used in this pamphlet are explained in the glossary.

Chapter 2
Military Problem and Components of the Solution

2-1. Military problem

a. Intelligence must provide commanders at all echelons, in all operational environments, the information and intelligence to enable operational adaptability as described in the ACC.

b. To meet the ACC requirement for operational adaptability in a constantly changing intelligence environment, intelligence must enhance existing and develop new capabilities to optimize intelligence support to "center of gravity" formations, defined as brigade combat teams (BCT) for irregular warfare and division and corps for major combat operations. Intelligence organizational enhancement must provide embedded, modular, full spectrum intelligence operations capabilities at every echelon, sustainable throughout the readiness cycle. The unprecedented increase in certification, licensing, and new equipment training generated by the expansion of biometrics, forensics, document and media exploitation, as well as SIGINT and HUMINT functions conducted at the company level requires significant training and equipment management expertise (not necessarily available at the BCT level).

c. TRADOC PAM 525-2-1 problem statement: How does the Army conduct synchronized, proactive intelligence operations to collect, analyze, continually reassess, and disseminate relevant information and actionable intelligence to help the future force understand adaptive threats in a complex operating environment in width, depth, and breadth and mitigate strategic, operational, and tactical uncertainty while supporting distributed, decentralized, full-spectrum operations and commander's decisionmaking?

2-2. Solution synopsis

a. TRADOC Pam 525-2-1 central idea. Develop adaptive Soldiers and leaders, within multifunctional organizations sustainable during persistent conflict, capable of conducting synchronized, proactive intelligence operations focused on BCT, division, and corps-level requirements to support planning and execution of distributed and decentralized full-spectrum operations.

b. Create versatile, expeditionary, agile, sustainable, and interoperable intelligence organizations capable of conducting synchronized, proactive intelligence operations. A campaign-capable expeditionary force is vital to meeting the demands of an environment of persistent conflict involving any combination of hierarchical, networked, and hybrid threats. In the near future, the Army will conduct continuous operations in this environment with a continuous demand for intelligence and information from collectors operating in the space, aerial, terrestrial, and foundational layer. These multifunctional organizations must be agile, able to be tailored as the tactical situation dictates. They must also be sustainable during persistent conflict.

(1) Establish and refine intelligence organizations to support situation development, provide targeting support and information superiority at the tactical level (for example, company intelligence support teams (CoIST)). The CoIST mission is to harvest local information and refine intelligence products provided by higher echelons to support company operations, disseminate and exchange information across all Army echelons and with joint, interagency, intergovernmental, multinational, nongovernmental, and host nation organizations to enable collaboration and unity of effort.

(2) Provide commanders the ability to pursue networked threat forces that emerge from reduced hierarchical military organizations. This requires task organization of intelligence, surveillance, and reconnaissance organizations to meet the commanders' future information collection and analysis needs. This flexibility is paramount to support the find, fix, finish, exploit, analyze, and disseminate (F3EAD) methodology.

c. Develop Soldiers and leaders. Future intelligence leaders will be required to support offensive, defensive, and stability or civil support operations simultaneously against both conventional and unconventional enemies. The future requires Soldiers and leaders with flexible mindsets who can work through ambiguity, and have the ability to conceptualize information and employ skills gained through lifelong learning. They must be capable of planning and conducting intelligence operations in accordance with the commander's intent in changing and ambiguous situations. Leaders will require the capability to recognize when operational and tactical situations require nonstandard solutions derived from assessment and creative thinking.

(1) Education. Intelligence analysts and leaders must possess a balance of cognitive, behavioral, and social skills. The future OE demands a clear set of leader development criteria for training, operational assignments, and self-development.

(2) Critical thinking. Intelligence analysts and leaders must be trained to possess the key abilities, characteristics, knowledge, and skills to perform complex critical thinking and analysis to provide commanders detailed analysis.

(3) Cultural Sophistication. Intelligence analysts and leaders must move from being culturally aware to cultural understanding to overcome "mirror imaging" (viewing the adversary through one's own eyes), and must gain or improve understanding on cultural differences, geography, patterns of thought, and mind sets.

d. Improve operations and intelligence synergy. Synchronized operations between operators and their intelligence personnel promote shared understanding, intent, and anticipatory intelligence, surveillance, and reconnaissance activities and limits collection and analysis of superfluous information. To produce a holistic, coordinated approach to intelligence, surveillance, and reconnaissance, the warfighting functions must be inextricably linked through the common responsibility to describe the environment (context) based on the commander's decisionmaking and information requirements.

(1) Co-creation of context. To develop the situation through action, commanders employ intelligence collectors, analysts, and associated systems as part of combined arms maneuver and wide area security. *Co-creation of context is a continuous process in which commanders direct intelligence priorities to drive operations, and the intelligence that these operations produce causes commanders to refine operations based on an improved understanding of the situation.*[3] Continuous interplay between the various intelligence disciplines and units conducting operations requires intelligence professionals and operators to collaborate at the lowest level.[4] This continuous dialogue creates timely, relevant, and clear information upon which commanders base their plans, decisions, and orders.

(2) The commander provides the guidance and focus through commander's critical information requirements (CCIRs) that drive the operations and intelligence processes. The intelligence process operates continuously during all phases of the operations process to provide the constant intelligence essential to the operations process. The information collection process must be synchronized, as are all other operational events; the selection and application of collection systems to meet the commander's information requirements are definitive operational concerns during the planning and conduct of any operation. The integrating processes of intelligence preparation of the battlefield (IPB) and intelligence, surveillance, and reconnaissance are fundamental to the operation.

(3) Broader intelligence, surveillance, and reconnaissance synchronization is required. *Intelligence, surveillance, and reconnaissance synchronization is the task that accomplishes the following: analyzes information requirements and intelligence gaps; evaluates available assets internal and external to the organization; determines gaps in the use of those assets; recommends intelligence, surveillance, and reconnaissance assets controlled by the organization to collect on the CCIR; and submits requests for information for adjacent and higher collection support.*[5] Intelligence, surveillance, and reconnaissance integration and synchronization must address the full range of PMESII-PT elements across all knowledge sources. Leaders and planners must recognize that there is a troops-to-task limitation involved with emphasis or increased information requirements concerning economics and governance intelligence to support stability operations. Analytical production is a zero sum game; when collectors and analysts are working on economics and governance, the commander will have less information concerning the conventional and/or insurgent threat, and less information to support kinetic targeting. When the operational focus is directed toward economic and governance activity, the collection and analysis of information from every soldier as a sensor must be focused on economic and governance activity; it is not enough to direct the traditional intelligence systems to collect and analyze data concerning the PMESII-PT factors. Rather, all elements of an organization must be considered coequal cohorts in the co-creation of context.

e. Develop collection, processing, exploitation, and dissemination capabilities to "see into" complex and urban environments. Future Army forces will conduct operations within a more complex environment. The Army must develop sensors to collect against signatures of threat and or interest in complex and urban terrain environments. Additionally the processing, exploitation, and dissemination of intelligence information is required to limit the latency in providing answers to the CCIRs.

f. Develop analytical capacity and capability. The Army's increased ability to detect threats from multiple sources requires an increased capability to receive, analyze, store, retrieve, manipulate, display, share, and communicate enormous volumes of information and intelligence within a secure and adaptable network. Likewise, data required for intelligence to support operations concerning stability, economic and governance (PMESII-PT) come from multiple sources not traditionally used by the intelligence systems. The ability to fuse all of the environmental factors into a single product is a multidisciplined process in which all the warfighting functions share responsibility; the combined effort in the co-creation of context is a commander-centric holistic endeavor that spans the entire spectrum of information management. The Army must train and develop intelligence analysts throughout the intelligence enterprise to ensure that they possess the key abilities, characteristics, knowledge, and skills to perform complex critical thinking necessary to provide commanders detailed analysis.

g. Leverage and extend the intelligence enterprise. The Army should not seek to replicate intelligence capabilities better resourced and executed by joint combat support agencies, and interagency counterparts. During deployment and redeployment, intelligence Soldiers, leaders, and units can remain connected to the intelligence enterprise through the Generating Force, national agencies (DOD and non-DOD) and theater capabilities. Knowledge centers provide the operational and tactical intelligence forces an interface and exchange of intelligence data and products with national, state, local, joint, Army, and partner nation databases and products. These architectures enable collaboration among strategic, operational, and tactical intelligence organizations in the following areas: intelligence reach; collaborative analysis; data storage, processing, and analysis; and intelligence production. Lessons learned from recent military operations have highlighted the need for increased intelligence capabilities within BCTs, maneuver battalions, and the maneuver company echelon. The extension of the intelligence enterprise to the lowest tactical echelon provides the capability to harvest local information and share it with adjacent and higher echelons.

(1) During predeployment preparations, intelligence Soldiers, leaders, and units increase their intelligence operations capabilities by leveraging the core analytical enterprise and the core processing, exploitation, and dissemination enterprise, enabled by cloud computing, to enhance readiness and add capacity by operating in support of deployed units. This is referred to as the exercise of tactical over watch.

(2) During deployment, units use reach to stay connected to Generating Force intelligence assets such as national agencies (DOD and non-DOD), and theater capabilities. These architectures enable collaboration among strategic, operational, and tactical intelligence organizations in the following areas: collaborative analysis; data storage, processing, and analysis; and intelligence production.

2-3. Future force Army intelligence components of the solution

a.   The future Army intelligence force must be organized, trained, and equipped to be tactically, operationally, and strategically mobile. Acknowledging that intelligence serves to improve the commander's understanding of the situation to make decisions, intelligence Soldiers, leaders, and units must be able to support commanders from the joint task force to company level. Successful mission command requires operational adaptability. Operational adaptability is essential for developing situational understanding and seizing, retaining, and exploiting the initiative. Intelligence, surveillance, and reconnaissance are indispensable in achieving operational adaptability. In some situations, sufficient current intelligence exists to plan and execute operations. In other situations, the conduct of reconnaissance is required to define the environment with sufficient resolution to plan and conduct operations. This is the essence of the operations and intelligence cycle.

b.   The Army intelligence force, as part of the intelligence enterprise, must operate across the full spectrum of operations in complex environments against hierarchical, networked, and hybrid threats. It must have the ability to operate in both multinational and multiple classification environments.

Chapter 3
Core Operational Actions

3-1. Introduction

a.   The ACC and AOC underscore the importance of intelligence in developing the commander's situational awareness and understanding. To develop the situation through action, commanders employ intelligence collectors, analysts, and associated systems as part of combined arms maneuver and wide area security. Continuous interplay between the various intelligence disciplines and units conducting operations requires intelligence professionals and operators to collaborate at the lowest level.[6] Intelligence Soldiers, access to data and analysis, and organizational agility (higher, lower, lateral) are critical to mitigating uncertainty and to improving the commander's situational understanding. The goal of intelligence is to provide commanders with critical information (such as, PMESII-PT) to support decisionmaking. This goal is achieved by providing intelligence about the adversary and the operational environment prior to engaging in operations and in all subsequent operations to execute missions effectively across full-spectrum operations and continuously during the operation.

b.   This construct of intelligence operation is very well within the scope of "fighting for information" and "developing the situation through action." Fighting for information is not synonymous with lethal or direct fire operations. Fighting for information begins with effective reconnaissance and intelligence collection to fill in the gaps in commanders' understanding of the situation. Fighting for information will require combined arms capabilities, access to joint capabilities, specialized training, and the employment of appropriate combinations of manned and unmanned air and ground systems. Understanding the enemy and the environment will require forces to see, fight, and learn across the depth and breadth of the AO. Changes in the OE are recorded to develop a predictive assessment.

c. Intelligence assists the commander in visualizing the operational environment, organizing forces, and controlling operations to achieve the desired objectives or end-state(s). Intelligence supports situational understanding throughout operations by continuously assessing reactions of the adversary and changes in the OE as well as the end-state results of operations. Intelligence also assists the commander in conducting other specialized missions such as incident awareness and assessment, site exploitation, attacking the transport layer, countering WMD, electronic warfare, cyber warfare, indications and warning, and security operations. Intelligence support is critical to target development and the targeting process and enables friendly forces the freedom of maneuver, to occupy or protect key terrain and engage the full range of target sets from enemy formations to key individuals.

d. Signal units support intelligence units by extending established transport layers to connect intelligence staffs and collection assets at various stages of the operations to enable access to actionable intelligence across all intelligence disciplines. Where necessary, signal elements establish new communications paths to meet unique demands of the mission. The intelligence enterprise approach integrates organizations, people, processes, and information from multiple entities and functions into a unified and highly dynamic activity. Each organization's intelligence capabilities (collection, processing, and analysis) support its internal members, but can support subordinate, lateral, and higher members. Enterprise interdependencies exist for integration and synchronization of intelligence collection, collaboration, analysis, processing, dissemination, and transport layering. Effective management of the enterprise capabilities enable every enterprise member from National, state, local, joint, Army, allied, tribal, and coalition to contribute to intelligence enterprise support to the commander(s).

e. Meeting operating environment challenges requires a foundational set of intelligence disciplines. These required disciplines are; CI, HUMINT, GEOINT, MASINT, OSINT, SIGINT, TECHINT, all-source intelligence and intelligence, surveillance, and reconnaissance synchronization. For purposes of this concept and current operations, police intelligence is also addressed. The Army may not be able to provide every identified capability requirement due to resource constraints and the physical environment in which future Army forces may operate. Therefore, prioritization is given to those capabilities which are paramount to successful intelligence operations. The selection of dedicated collection systems must reflect the enemy situation and support the commander's information requirements. Asset management is a task organization and operational decision. Intelligence forces at echelons BCT through Army service component command (ASCC), in both the active and reserve components, require the capabilities outlined below. Appendixes B through D provide a detailed listing of all required future Army forces capabilities by intelligence discipline.

3-2. Conduct security force assistance

a. The operational environment will be extremely fluid, with continually changing coalitions, alliances, partnerships, and actors. U.S. national security and defense strategies will depend on strong foreign and local ties. Through these interagency and foreign defense relationships, the

U.S. not only helps avert crises, but also improves its effectiveness in responding to these crises. Building trust and relationships will be keys to responding to future crises, but the U.S. cannot simply "surge" trust and relationship on demand; these must be developed and maintained over time. Intelligence units will provide unique support to Army commanders to partner with foreign security forces, homeland defense (state, local, and tribal), Federal, allied, and coalition entities. This support will include both indirect (such as, multinational exercises, exchange programs, selected joint exercises, and others) and direct (intelligence support to U.S. commanders).

b. The focus of intelligence support to security force assistance is to develop trained, resilient, and legitimate foreign intelligence security forces that are able to maintain a secure environment. Within the range of security cooperation activities, the most dynamic in the coming years will be security force assistance missions: "hands on" efforts conducted primarily in host countries, to train, equip, advise, and assist those countries forces in becoming more proficient at providing security. These security force assistance activities can help enable host nation participation in coalition stability operations and multilateral peacekeeping operations that improve regional security. Building partner capacity by increasing future Army forces security force assistance capabilities, including linguistic, regional, and cultural expertise, will help prevent conflict and reduce the demands on U.S. forces over the long term. Intelligence support will focus on the capabilities specified below to support security force assistance missions.

(1) Providing advisors to plan and conduct intelligence training for security force assistance.

(2) Providing assistance to the counterpart in developing a local intelligence collection program.

(3) Providing assistance in evaluating the foreign intelligence staff, its standard operating procedures, its chain of command, intelligence projects, and reference material available from other intelligence agencies.

(4) Establishing combined cells for intelligence, operations, planning, and sustainment.

(5) Providing intelligence support to security force assistance to host nation and U.S. Army commanders.

(6) Providing assistance on criminal activities intelligence.

(7) Providing intelligence to commanders at the "tactical edge" conducting decentralized operations.

(8) Disseminating, sharing, and exchanging intelligence across all Army echelons and joint, interagency, intergovernmental, multinational, nongovernmental, and host nation organizations to enable collaboration and unity of effort.

(9) Establishing information and aggressive intelligence sharing between partners using existing transport layers.

(10) Establishing and/or continuing foreign officer training at U.S. Army schools.

3-3. Shaping and entry operations

a. Shaping operations. Shaping operations create and preserve conditions for the successful planning and execution of decisive operations. Shaping operations include fires activities conducted throughout the AO. They support the decisive operation by affecting adversary capabilities and forces, or by influencing adversary decisions (such as, through support to the deception plan). Intelligence analysis and intelligence, surveillance, and reconnaissance activities support the development and execution of shaping operations through the following.

(1) Identifying threat centers of gravity and decisive points on the battlefield.

(2) Providing the commander with economic, cultural, and political context of the AO.

(3) Providing likely response of the adversary and local populace to U.S. operations.

(4) Providing intelligence staffs (analysis) and supporting units (collection and analysis) at joint, corps, division and BCT also ensure the intelligence process focuses on the CCIRs to include priority intelligence requirements (PIR) and friendly force information requirements (FFIR).

(5) Providing predictive intelligence to give commanders time to understand how the adversary will react to U.S. courses of action (COAs) so that appropriate shaping operations can be implemented.

(6) Anticipating, identify, considering, and evaluating all threats to the entire unit.

(7) Providing accurate, timely, and detailed geographic information to include gaps, possible obstacles, and other terrain information that can restrict or affect the shaping operation.

(8) Providing intelligence to commanders at the "tactical edge" conducting decentralized operations.

(9) Disseminating, sharing, and exchanging intelligence across all Army echelons and joint, interagency, intergovernmental, multinational, nongovernmental, and host nation organizations to enable collaboration and unity of effort.

b. These factors are critical during the deployment and entry operations stages of force projection. During these stages, the unit is particularly vulnerable to adversary actions because of its limited combat power and knowledge of the AO. Intelligence personnel must, therefore, emphasize the delivery of combat information and intelligence products that indicate changes to the threat or AO developed during predeployment IPB.

c. Entry operations. Enemies often possess the motives and means to interrupt the deployment flow of Army forces. Threats to deploying forces may include advanced conventional weaponry (missiles, air defense, mines, and others), cyber attacks, and the use of WMD. Sea ports and air ports of embarkation and debarkation should be regarded as adversary high payoff targets because they are the entry points for forces and equipment. Ports of embarkation and/or debarkation are vulnerable because they are fixed targets with significant machinery and equipment that are vulnerable to attack. Military forces and materiel, host nation support personnel, contractors, and other civilians are more vulnerable at these locations.

d. Additionally, criminals sabotage critical materiel and supplies or steal them and try to sell them on the black market. In some cases, allied criminal elements may give stolen supplies to adversary forces. An adversary attack (physical or cyber) or even the threat of an adversary attack on a port of embarkation and/or debarkation can have a major impact on force projection momentum. Commanders at all levels require predictive and operational intelligence so that they may focus attention on security actions that reduce vulnerabilities. To avoid, neutralize, or counter threats to entry operations, commanders rely on the ability of intelligence forces to support future operations through the following:

(1) Identifying accurately adversary reactions to U.S. actions, anticipating their response to our counteractions, and predicting additional enemy COAs.

(2) Detecting and locating enemy antiaccess and area denial capabilities and identify enemy vulnerabilities that can be exploited by the maneuver.

(3) Providing the size, composition, structure, and deployment sequence of the enemy force to create the conditions for success.

(4) Identifying potential adversary decisions before the actual event.

(5) Providing en route intelligence access to the commander to address change significantly before execution.

(6) Providing intelligence to commanders at the tactical edge conducting decentralized operations.

(7) Disseminating, sharing, and exchanging intelligence across all Army echelons and joint, interagency, intergovernmental, multinational, nongovernmental, and host nation organizations to enable collaboration and unity of effort.

e. Intelligence must provide timely, accurate, and predictive intelligence to ensure the commander can retain the initiative to implement the plan or make decisions before losing the opportunity. Situational awareness and understanding derived from joint, interagency, intergovernmental, and multinational intelligence sources are critical during all phases but particularly during Phase 0 (shape) and Phase 1 (deter) as operational and tactical forces deploy, since organic collectors are not in range or have just recently arrived in theater. Army Generating Force intelligence capabilities depend on joint, interagency, intergovernmental, and multinational intelligence capabilities to develop and understand the OE and support operational and tactical forces.

3-4. Intertheater and intratheater operational maneuver

a. Intelligence support to intertheater and intratheater operational maneuver is provided by generating, operational, and tactical forces and includes establishing intelligence communications architecture; knowledge management to enable intelligence reach; collaborative analysis; data storage, processing, and analysis; and intelligence production between the strategic and operational parts of the IC.

b. Intelligence products portray the enemy and aspects of the environment and enable the commander to identify potential COAs, plan operations, employ forces and develop targeting guidance effectively in support of the movement and maneuver warfighting function.

c. In the conduct of shaping and follow-on entry operations, Army intelligence relies heavily on national, joint, allied, and coalition intelligence support until such time as Army forces actually establish a physical presence on the ground. At this point in the operation, the deployment and employment of the Army's close tactical collection capabilities begins to influence the conduct of subsequent operations. There will be instances where the nation has not made a significant investment in HUMINT assets in low priority countries or regions that suddenly become high priority. Collection efforts will rely primarily on whatever sources are available within country and on external technical collection capabilities the force can bring to bear until such time as Army forces close on the sea and air ports of debarkation. Collection and analytical assets in transit are of limited capability. Future maritime and airlift platforms should ideally be configured to support continued collection and analysis while in transit.

d. Intertheater maneuver is the maneuver over extended distances of aerial, ground, sea, high altitude, and space capabilities, to achieve a positional advantage over enemies. The goal of future intertheater maneuver is to enable the movement of sufficient combat power and sustainment from garrisons, through intermediate staging base if necessary, directly into action. The goals of Army intelligence as applied to intertheater operational maneuver are the following:

(1) Detecting and locating enemy antiaccess and area denial capabilities and identify enemy vulnerabilities that can be exploited through maneuver.

(2) Providing Generating Force intelligence capabilities and drawing on intelligence organizations within and outside the DOD to understand the OE and support operational and tactical forces.

(3) Providing timely, actionable intelligence which enables friendly forces to occupy or protect key terrain and facilities.

(4) Identifying areas from which friendly forces can repel enemy forces or secure populations and continue the flow of follow-on forces.

(5) Providing intelligence to commanders at the "tactical edge" conducting decentralized operations.

(6) Disseminating, sharing, and exchanging intelligence across all Army echelons and joint, interagency, intergovernmental, multinational, nongovernmental, and host nation organizations to enable collaboration and unity of effort.

(7) Detecting, identifying, and locating enemy supporting space-based intelligence, surveillance, and reconnaissance and communications capabilities and identifying their vulnerabilities that can be exploited.

e. Continuity and understanding is critical during all phases, but particularly during Phase 0 and Phase 1 as it is the principal source from which deploying (shaping and entry operations) operational and tactical forces initially rely, since organic collectors are not in range or are recently arrived.

f. Intratheater maneuver is the movement within a theater of aerial, ground, sea, high altitude, and space capabilities to achieve a positional advantage over enemies. Intratheater maneuver using platforms with sufficient speed and ability to land at unimproved, degraded, or less than optimal locations will mitigate risks posed by enemy antiaccess and area denial operations. The goals of Army intelligence as applied to intratheater operational maneuver are the following:

(1) Detecting, identifying, and locating enemy antiaccess and area denial capabilities.

(2) Providing intelligence on terrain and gaps.

(3) Identifying enemy vulnerabilities that may be exploited by the maneuver force.

(4) Providing intelligence to commanders at the tactical edge conducting decentralized operations.

(5) Disseminating, sharing, and exchanging intelligence across all Army echelons and joint, interagency, intergovernmental, multinational, nongovernmental, and host nation organizations to enable collaboration and unity of effort.

(6) Detecting, identifying, and locating enemy supporting space-based intelligence, surveillance, and reconnaissance and communications capabilities.

g. Future Army forces will also conduct intratheater maneuver to seize key terrain, secure populations, and to destroy enemy forces and capabilities in depth. To support these anticipated operations intelligence collection capabilities, both technical and human will need to evolve so that the enemy's ability to hide in urban or complex terrain is severely curtailed or even eliminated. Just as the military developed and fielded new night fighting capabilities in the early 1980s to "own the night," it must now develop the capabilities to "own the terrain" above and below ground.

3-5. Full-spectrum operations

a. Commanders use combined arms to increase the effects of combat power through complementary and reinforcing capabilities. Combined arms merge leadership, information, and each of the warfighting functions and their supporting systems. Used destructively, combined arms integrate different capabilities so that counteracting one makes the enemy vulnerable to another. Used constructively, combined arms multiply the effectiveness and the efficiency of Army capabilities used in stability or civil support operations. The nature of combined arms operations is changing or broadening beyond the construct in which the Army normally thinks of what makes combined arms operations. Historically, combined arms operations were regarded as those involving primarily infantry, armor, artillery, and aviation assets. The modern construct requires that the Army think in a much broader context and include force multipliers such as space and cyber operations in the conduct of combined arms operations. Future combined arms operations could be conducted by specialty brigades as well as BCTs, and employ soft or nonlethal capabilities that may never result in a single shot being fired during a successful engagement. Intelligence is involved in either the conduct of or support of these types of soft, nonlethal engagements on a continual basis globally in support of national agencies and combatant commanders. These types of combined arms activities serve to support long-term strategic shaping activities as well as support ongoing tactical level operations in the current fight.

b. Intelligence is a continuous full spectrum combined arms activity led by the intelligence staffs and is always engaged in supporting the commander in full-spectrum operations at joint, corps and division, BCT, battalion, and maneuver company levels to ensure the intelligence process focuses on the CCIRs (PIRs and FFIRs). For instance, the corps and division headquarters (HQ) would receive its collection support from a supporting battlefield surveillance brigade and other theater MI brigade (which also supports the ASCC). The BCT through company would receive their primary support through organic intelligence staffs and units. In the future, environment intelligence must maintain the capability to perform the following:

(1) Provide products that are timely, relevant, accurate, and predictive.

(2) Provide intelligence to full-spectrum operations on no or limited notice.

(3) Conduct realistic training, thorough planning, meticulous preparation, and aggressive execution posture.

(4) Provide intelligence to commanders at the tactical edge conducting decentralized operations.

(5) Disseminate, share, and exchange intelligence across all Army echelons and joint, interagency, intergovernmental, multinational, nongovernmental, and host nation organizations to enable collaboration and unity of effort.

c. This support is comprehensive and reaches across full-spectrum operations and levels of war to produce the intelligence required to accomplish the mission successfully. A combination of space, aerial (low, mid, and high altitude), seaborne, ground-based systems, and HUMINT capabilities provide the most comprehensive intelligence picture possible. During force projection operations, intelligence supports the commander with accurate and responsive intelligence from predeployment through redeployment.

d. The intelligence architecture provides specific intelligence and communications structures at each echelon from the strategic level through the tactical level. These structures include intelligence organizations, systems, and procedures for collecting, processing, analyzing, and disseminating intelligence and other critical information in a useable form to those in need, when in need. Effective communications connectivity, multilevel security, and automation are essential components of this architecture. Additionally, future Army forces require the capability to continue intelligence operations when the network is degraded or compromised. All military forces, including Army and Army special operations forces (ARSOF), have benefited from the increase in intelligence, surveillance, and reconnaissance capabilities, most notably unmanned aircraft systems (UAS). However, platforms alone are not sufficient. To be effective, information obtained from the "unblinking eye" (that is, persistent surveillance) must be processed, exploited, and disseminated, which requires intelligence analysts and communications systems (a dedicated, multidisciplined, all-source intelligence effort), including sufficient bandwidth, to disseminate the intelligence.

e. Irregular warfare, including counterinsurgency, as a part of whole-of-government effort, requires a combined arms approach emphasizing small unit capabilities and coordination with ongoing ARSOF operations in cooperation with host nation and interagency organizations. There are principally five activities or operations undertaken in campaigns to address irregular threats: counterterrorism, unconventional warfare, foreign internal defense, counterinsurgency, and stability operations. In addition to these five core activities, there are a host of key related activities including strategic communication, IO of all kinds, psychological operations, civil-military operations, and support to law enforcement, intelligence, and counterintelligence operations in which the Army may engage to counter irregular threats.

f. To maximize the prospect of success, the intelligence warfighting function must incorporate an understanding of the population and operating environment, including the complex historical, political, sociocultural, religious, economic, and other causes of violent conflict. The Army must adopt collaborative frameworks to understand, plan, act, assess, and adapt in concert with U.S. Government interagency and multinational partners and the host nation. Furthermore, requirements that characterize counterinsurgency in general, and civil security and civil control in particular, vary significantly among tactical-level areas of operations. This situation requires releasing intelligence, civil affairs, and information assets typically held at higher HQ to BCTs and often to battalion task forces.

g. The top priority of the DOD is to protect and defend the homeland. Homeland defense and civil support operations help ensure the integrity and security of the homeland by detecting, deterring, preventing, or if necessary, defeating threats and aggression against the U.S. as early and as far from its borders as possible so as to minimize their effects on U.S. society and interests. The DOD and the Army also may be directed to assist civilian authorities in the U.S. to save lives, protect property, enhance public health and safety, or to lessen or avert the threat of a catastrophe. The DOD provides many unique capabilities that can be used to mitigate and manage the consequences of natural and manmade disasters and must be prepared to provide support to Federal, state, and local authorities.

3-6. Conduct overlapping protection operations

a. Protection operations consist of those actions taken to prevent or mitigate hostile actions against DOD personnel (to include DA civilians, contractors, uniformed personnel, and family members), resources, facilities, and critical information. Future Army forces may also be required to extend protection capabilities to the local population, to host nation security and military forces, to multinational partners, to interagency partners, and to other friendly organizations in the area of operations. These actions include the following:

(1) Conserving the force's fighting potential for application at the decisive time and place.

(2) Incorporating coordinated and synchronized offensive and defensive measures.

(3) Facilitating the effective employment of the joint force while degrading the capabilities of and opportunities for the threat.

(4) Maintaining awareness of policies for intelligence support to homeland security.

(5) Providing intelligence to commanders at the "tactical edge" conducting decentralized operations.

(6) Disseminate, share, and exchange intelligence across all Army echelons and joint, interagency, intergovernmental, multinational, nongovernmental, and host nation organizations to enable collaboration and unity of effort.

b. Intelligence support to protection operations consists of monitoring and reporting the activities, intentions, and capabilities of adversarial groups and determining their possible COAs. Detecting the adversary's methods in today's OE requires a higher level of situational understanding, informed by current and precise intelligence. This type of threat drives the need for predictive intelligence based on analysis of focused information from intelligence, law enforcement, and security activities. Effective integration of counterintelligence operations and protection operations will significantly enhance mission effectiveness.

c. Intelligence analysis in support of protection operations employs analytical methodologies and tools to provide situational understanding and to predict the adversary's actions. Modified or standard time-event charts, association matrixes, activity matrixes, link diagrams, and overlays are beneficial in monitoring the actions of the adversary. Link analysis is the process of identifying and analyzing relationships between personnel, contacts, associations, events, activities, organizations, and transport layers to determine key and/or significant links. Overlays may include (but are not limited to) threat training camps, organizations, finances, personalities, industrial sites, information systems, decisionmaking infrastructures, specific activities, and locations of previous attacks.

3-7. Distributed support and sustainment

a. Distributed support and sustainment of forces involves providing levels of required support across extended distances and multiple locations. Sustainment of forces requires dramatic improvements in fuels, power generation, water production, and improved reliability, availability, and maintainability. Movement of intelligence elements is accomplished using advanced intratheater and intertheater sealift and airlift platforms capable of delivering intelligence forces to the point of need in a roll-off-the-ramp configuration.

b. Intelligence support to distributed support and sustainment operations involves providing intelligence support across extended distances and multiple locations. Sustainment forces require intelligence support to enable successful sustainment operations. Sustainment forces require access to the same intelligence information and resources as maneuver forces commensurate with the lethality of the environment. This intelligence support ranges from situational awareness on lethal to cyber threats, to include potential adversary deception operations against the sustainment system.

3-8. Network-enabled mission command

a. Mission command is the exercise of authority and direction by commanders, supported by their staffs, using the art of command and the science of control to integrate warfighting functions in the conduct of full-spectrum operations. Mission command uses mission orders to ensure disciplined initiative within the commander's intent, enabling agile and adaptive commanders, leaders, and organizations. Successful mission command demands that subordinate leaders at all echelons exercise disciplined initiative, act aggressively, and independently to accomplish the mission within the commander's intent. Mission command gives subordinates the greatest possible freedom of action. Mission command supports design. Commanders focus their orders on the purpose of the operation rather than on the details of how to perform assigned tasks. They delegate most decisions to subordinates. This minimizes detailed control and empowers subordinates' initiative.

b. Mission command emphasizes timely decisionmaking, understanding the higher commander's intent, and clearly identifying the subordinates' tasks necessary to achieve the desired end state. It improves the subordinates' ability to act effectively in fluid, chaotic situations. Intelligence is the Army's principal tool to mitigate uncertainty and brings clarity to chaotic situations thereby enabling effective mission command. Mission command details three supporting ideas: empower the lowest possible echelon, develop expertise in the art of design as well as in the other components of the operations process, and educate and train the force for uncertain and complex operational environments.

c. To support mission command in the 2016-2028 timeframe, intelligence operations must further integrate organizations, people, processes, and information from multiple entities and functions into a unified and highly dynamic activity. This activity must enable both its personnel and organizations to operate effectively and efficiently. Current and future intelligence units must possess the organic capabilities of collection, processing, access, analysis, and dissemination. These organic capabilities support future mission command at subordinate, lateral, and higher levels under increased conditions of uncertainty. Interdependencies exist now and will increase in the future for integration and synchronization of intelligence collection, collaboration, analysis, processing, dissemination, and transport layering between all echelons. There will be an increased demand for analysts to perform PMESII-PT analysis at both static locations and while commanders and staffs are on the move. Effective management of intelligence capabilities will enable intelligence operations from national, joint, Army, allied, and coalition organizations to contribute to intelligence support to mission command at all levels in both centralized and decentralized operations and facilitate the sharing of information with joint, interagency, intergovernmental, and multinational partners.

d. Signal units support intelligence units with extended transport layers to connect intelligence staffs and collection assets at various stages of the operations. This is accomplished by using multidomain, terrestrial, aerial (low, medium, high altitude), and space-based communications networks for movement of intelligence throughout the battlespace. Where necessary, signal units establish new communications paths to meet unique demands of the mission. The theater, corps, division, and BCTs' analysis and control elements play a critical role in making communications paths, transport layers, and intelligence databases available to maneuver forces. The reliance on transport layered systems will result in greater emphasis being placed on information assurance. Additionally, intelligence organizations must establish tactics, techniques, and procedures for operating when the transport layer is degraded due to system failure, natural disaster, or enemy action. The primary and alternate transport layer connections are critical to support mission command under periods of degraded operations.

e. The Army future force must implement a new strategy to ensure development and sustainment of intelligence analytic continuity across multiple theaters and multiple unit rotations. This is critical to intelligence support of mission command in the future operating environment. Establishment of habitual unit associations and infrastructure enhancement (for example, the Striker BCT intelligence operations facility at Fort Lewis, WA) will facilitate future development and sustain intelligence continuity and support to mission command in the future.

Chapter 4
Conclusion

4-1. Summary

a. The Army must determine the most probable types of conflict it will be asked to support in the future. Further, it must determine when and where these conflicts will most likely occur and the likely major components of the conflict (such as, war among the people, nation-state on nation-state, or some combination).

b. Future Army forces, including intelligence forces, must maintain a proper balance of moral, physical, and cognitive development with contributions from science and technology that can enhance Soldier physical and mental performance. Further, intelligence organizations need the depth of expertise to sustain cross discipline technical training and leader development throughout a force generation cycle. Future conflict will remain complex and chaotic, and human frailties and irrationality will continue to characterize war's nature. Uncertainty, danger, physical exertion, friction, and chance constitute the climate of war, which contributes to the fog of war with which commanders must contend in future operations. Intelligence (both technological and human), and operational design can and will mitigate uncertainty. However, commanders must still make decisions based on voluminous data, some of which will be incomplete, inaccurate, or contradictory. These factors will continue to play a predominant role in the environment of future full-spectrum operations.

c. The Army capabilities based assessment solution strategy for intelligence must address several fundamental conditions in the future:

(1) A decentralized operation increases the intelligence capabilities required at the lower echelons.

(2) Analyst organization and utilization must be modified to meet projected future OE.

(3) There will be an increased demand for regional intelligence expertise.

(4) There will be an increased demand for analysts to perform PMESII-PT analysis.

(5) Intelligence support to nonlethal operations among the people demands greater precision and continuity of support to the commander.

(6) Management of intelligence collection, analysis, and production will be coordinated across echelons and partners to ensure unity of effort.

(7) Operations dominated by urban and complex terrain will require a combination of existing and new technical sensors and expanded HUMINT capacity to exploit previously unexploited spectrums and/or signatures to "see into" complex and urban terrain.

(8) The intelligence enterprise must be manned and equipped with appropriate skill sets.

(9) There will be a requirement to retain and sustain key skills to avoid limited reconstitution time.

(10) Exploitation of previously collected data (for example imagery and forensic data) is critical to timely targeting and support to the maneuver commander.

(11) Acquisition of Army intelligence hardware and software is challenged by the rapid pace of technological change, driven by commercial industry.

d. The TRADOC PAM 525-2-1 solution strategy for the 2016-2028 OE must possess both evolutionary (low risk with linear increase in capability) and revolutionary (high risk and/or high dollar action with exponential increase in capability) intelligence components. Due to the constraints of budget, demographics, organizational and personnel acquisition changes, these will normally be evolutionary efforts.

e. A set of intelligence DOTMLPF considerations for the future OE is contained in appendix F.

4-2. Closing

Timely and effective intelligence is a precursor to all successful operations across the spectrum of conflict and operational themes. "Effective maneuver and fires require timely, accurate intelligence" and intelligence has the task to support the commander's situational understanding.[7] Intelligence enables effective mission command by leveraging intelligence, reconnaissance, and surveillance, to provide situational awareness and to enable positional advantage. As such, intelligence is inextricably linked to supporting maneuver and fires in operational and tactical operations. Commanders drive intelligence. Intelligence drives all operations, never breaks contact, and is never finished.

Appendix A
References
ARs, DA Pams, field manuals (FM), and DA forms are available at Army Publishing Directorate (APD) Home Page http://www.usapa.army.mil. TRADOC publications and forms are available at TRADOC Publications at http://www.tradoc.army.mil.

Section I
Required Publications

TRADOC Operational Environment 2009-2025

TRADOC Pam 525-3-0
The Army Capstone Concept, Operational Adaptability: Operating Under Conditions of Uncertainty and Complexity in an Era of Persistent Conflict, 2016-2028

TRADOC Pam 525-3-1
The U.S. Army Operating Concept 2016-2028

Section II
Related Publications

2008 National Defense Strategy. Retrieved from http://www.defense.gov/pubs/2008 NationalDefenseStrategy.pdf

Bringing Intelligence About, Practitioners Reflect on Best Practices. (2003, May). Center for Strategic Intelligence Research, Joint Military Intelligence College. Available by permission from https://www.us.army.mil\suite\portal\index.jsp

DOD 5240.1-R
Procedures Governing the Activities of DOD Intelligence Components that affect U.S. Persons.

DOD Directive (DODD) 5240.1
DOD Intelligence Activities

DODD 5525.5
DOD Cooperation with Civilian Law Enforcement Officials

DOD Deterrence Operations, Joint Operating Concept

DOD Homeland Defense and Civil Support Joint Operating Concept

DOD Major Combat Operations Joint Operating Concept

DOD Quadrennial Defense Review Report. (2010, February 1). Washington DC. Retrieved from http://www.defense.gov/qdr/

Executive Order 12333
U.S. Intelligence Activities

Flynn, M., Pottinger, M., & Batchelor, P. (2010, January). Fixing intel: A blueprint for making intelligence relevant in Afghanistan. *Voices from the Field*. Center for a New American Security. Washington, D.C. Retrieved from http://www.cnas.org/files/documents/publications/ AfghanIntel_Flynn_Jan2010_code507_voices.pdf

FM 2-0
Intelligence

FM 2-19.4
Brigade Combat Team Intelligence Operations

FM 2-01.3
Intelligence Preparation of the Battlefield/Battlespace

FM 2-22.2
Counterintelligence

FM 2-22.3
Human Intelligence Collector Operations

FM 2-91.4
Intelligence Support to Urban Operations

FM 2-22.401
Multi-Service Tactics, Techniques, and Procedures for Technical Intelligence Operations

FM 3-0
Operations

FM 4-0
Sustainment

FM 3-55.1
Battlefield Surveillance Brigade

Joint Publication (JP) 3-28
Civil Support

Military Intelligence Vision Statement. (2007, November). Retrieved from https:// www.us.army.mil\suite\portal\index.jsp

Theater intelligence, surveillance, and reconnaissance concept of operations. (2008, January 4). Retrieved from https://www.us.army.mil\suite\portal\index.jsp.

TRADOC Pam 525-2-1
The United States Army Functional Concept for Intelligence 2016-2028

TRADOC Pam 525-3-3
The United States Army Functional Concept for Mission Command 2016-2028

TRADOC Pam 525-3-4
The United States Army Functional Concept for Fires 2016-2028

TRADOC Pam 525-3-6
The United States Army Functional Concept for Movement and Maneuver 2016-2028

TRADOC Pam 525-3-7
Army Concept for the Human Dimension in Full Spectrum Operations 2015-2024

TRADOC Pam 525-3-7-01
Army Study of the Human Dimension in the Future 2015-2024

TRADOC Pam 525-4-1
The United States Army Functional Concept for Sustainment 2016-2028

TRADOC Pam 525-7-9
The U.S. Army's Concept Capability Plan, Intelligence, Surveillance, and Reconnaissance, 2015-2024.

TRADOC Pamphlet 525-66
Force Operating Capabilities

U.S. Army Intelligence Center Requirements Determination Directorate. (2007, August). The Army Comprehensive Intelligence Guide to Modularity, 3.0. Available by permission from https://icon.army.mil/MCAT/documents/filemanager.cfm

United States Joint Forces Command Joint Operating Environment. (2010 February 18). Retrieved from http://www.fjcom.mil/newslink/storyarchive/2010/JOE_o.pdf

U.S. Northern Command (USNORTHCOM). Homeland Defense Concept of Employment. (2004 July 16). Retrieved from https://www.us.army.mil\suite\portal\index.jsp

U.S. Special Operations Command, Capstone Concept for Special Operations. (2006). Retrieved from https://www.us.army.mil\suite\portal\index.jsp

Appendix B
Required Capabilities

B-1. ACC intelligence required capabilities

a. Combined arms, air-ground reconnaissance. Future Army forces must be capable of conducting combined arms, air-ground reconnaissance operations that integrate long-range surveillance capabilities and HUMINT collection to overcome countermeasures, develop the situation, and assist commanders in making decisions.

b. Combined information sources. Future Army forces require the capability to access all data and information in an integrated form from numerous collection assets to develop the intelligence and degree of understanding necessary for successful operations against enemy organizations in complex environments.

c. Interagency intelligence capabilities. Commanders must have access to complementary interagency capabilities (for example, police and criminal investigation skills, national level intelligence analysis, institutional development skills, financial expertise, and expertise in the rule of law) to understand the situation and initiate appropriate actions and programs.

d. Tactical intelligence collection and analysis. Future Army forces require the capability to push analysis capabilities and relevant intelligence products down to lower tactical elements (company and platoon, and possibly below based on the situation) to maximize the combat effectiveness of small units and allow tactical commanders to develop the situation further through action.

e. Develop and optimize collection and analytical capabilities. Future Army forces require access to and direction of advanced information and intelligence collection and analytical capabilities across the seven doctrinal intelligence disciplines and other nontraditional sources (for example, biometric and forensic capabilities, civil affairs elements, liaisons, interagency and nongovernmental organizations, psychological operations teams, and human terrain teams) at lower tactical elements (company and possibly below based on the situation) to facilitate the situational understanding and timely decisionmaking required to seize and retain the initiative.

f. Broaden analysis beyond military focused intelligence preparation of the operational environment. Future Army forces require the capability at all echelons to conduct analysis of political, military, economic, sociological, infrastructure, and informational aspects of the OE, to develop a clear understanding of the operational environment.

B-2. AOC intelligence required capabilities

a. Future Army forces require the capability to conduct intelligence, surveillance, and reconnaissance synchronization from the national to the tactical level during full-spectrum operations to enable situational awareness and understanding.

b. Future Army forces require the capability to develop intelligence requirements in full-spectrum operations to satisfy commanders' information needs.

c. Future Army forces require the capability to provide advanced collection and analytical capabilities in sufficient numbers with requisite organizational flexibility, deployability, mobility, and sustainability to address changes within the OE and signatures of interest to develop the situation through action by acquiring precise and timely information.

d. Future Army forces require the capability to integrate knowledge of the theater environment, such as culture, terrain, weather, infrastructure, demographics, and neutral entities, in particular, understanding the perceptions of partners and other human elements of the environment to develop the situation through action and exert psychological and technical influence.

e. Future Army forces require the capability to conduct analysis of political, military, economic, sociological, infrastructure, and information aspects of the OE (and mission, enemy, troops, time available, terrain, and civil considerations (METT-TC), at all echelons to allow commanders at all levels to conduct decentralized operations in cooperation with partners while exerting psychological and technical influence.

f. Future Army forces require the capability to manage knowledge through the systematic process of discovering, selecting, organizing, distilling, sharing, developing, and using information in a social domain context to develop the situation through action.

g. Future Army forces require the capability to incorporate all sources of information and intelligence, including open-source information, and fuse and produce intelligence in the context of the joint operational environment, to include degraded conditions, to provide a holistic understanding of the adversary and the OE while conducting full-spectrum operations.

h. Future Army forces require the capability to support ARSOF unique intelligence, surveillance, reconnaissance, and reach requirements to ensure ARSOF can conduct its core missions.

i. Future Army forces require the capability to synchronize ARSOF units' intelligence and knowledge management capabilities to ensure full operational environment awareness.

B-3. First order required capabilities (what intelligence needs to do)

a. Future Army intelligence forces require the capability to develop in-depth understanding and anticipate the commander's information and intelligence requirements during full-spectrum operations to enhance operations and intelligence integration and provide intelligence that supports all levels of decisionmaking.

b. Future Army intelligence forces require the capability to leverage the enterprise (DOD, non-DOD) during full-spectrum operations to access all pertinent information and intelligence to support decisionmaking.

c. Future Army intelligence forces require the capability to provide flexible organizational designs that are rapidly deployable and highly sustainable during full-spectrum operations to provide the commander intelligence that supports targeting and decisionmaking.

d. Future Army intelligence forces require the capability to establish continuous situational awareness (identify and locate adversary) in and out of contact before, during, and after a campaign to provide an overall picture of the adversary and the OE.

e. Future Army intelligence forces require the capability to capitalize on technological advances (technical insertions) in collection, analysis, processing, dissemination, information, and intelligence during full-spectrum operations to provide the commander intelligence that supports targeting and decisionmaking.

f. Future Army intelligence forces require the capability to collect, analyze, process, disseminate information and intelligence on-the-move to provide the commander intelligence that supports targeting and decisionmaking.

g. Future Army intelligence forces require the capability to provide analytical capabilities and access at the lowest practical level during full-spectrum operations to provide the commander intelligence that supports local situational awareness, targeting, and decisionmaking.

h. Future Army intelligence forces require the capability to detect signatures utilizing a mix of intelligence sensors (human and/or technical) at all echelons during full-spectrum operations to provide the commander intelligence that supports situational awareness, targeting, and decisionmaking.

i. Future Army intelligence forces require the capability to conduct intelligence, surveillance, and reconnaissance synchronization during all operations to answer the commander's PIRs, and CCIRs, to support the commander's situational understanding of the operational environment and adversary.

j. Future Army intelligence forces require the capability to conduct IPB to understand the environment in which the future Army finds itself and understands the perceptions of partners and the other human elements of the environment.

k. Future Army intelligence forces require the capability to provide intelligence support under degraded network conditions during full-spectrum operations to provide the commander intelligence that supports situational awareness, targeting, and decisionmaking.

B-4. Second order: what intelligence needs from other warfighting functions

a. Mission command.

(1) Future Army intelligence forces require the capability to integrate commander's intent and guidance with intelligence collection, planning, and analysis to enhance operations and intelligence integration and provide intelligence that supports all levels of decisionmaking.

(2) Future Army intelligence forces require the capability to integrate commander's PIR with intelligence collection, planning, and analysis to enhance operations and intelligence integration and provide intelligence that supports all levels of decisionmaking.

(3) Future Army intelligence forces require the capability to integrate every soldier as sensor information with intelligence collection, planning, and analysis to enhance operations and intelligence integration and provide intelligence that supports all levels of decisionmaking.

b. Movement and maneuver.

(1) Future Army intelligence forces require the capability to integrate movement and maneuver sensors and activity results with intelligence collection planning and analysis to enhance operations and intelligence integration and provide intelligence that supports all levels of decisionmaking.

(2) Future Army intelligence forces require the capability to integrate every soldier as sensor information with intelligence collection, planning, and analysis to enhance operations and intelligence integration and provide intelligence that supports all levels of decisionmaking

c. Fires.

(1) Future Army intelligence forces require the capability to integrate target acquisition sensors with intelligence collection, planning, and analysis to enhance operations and intelligence integration and provide intelligence that supports all levels of decisionmaking.

(2) Future Army intelligence forces require the capability to integrate high value targets and high payoff target lists into the intelligence collection, planning, and analysis to enhance operations and intelligence integration and provide intelligence that supports all levels of decisionmaking.

(3) Future Army intelligence forces require the capability to integrate every soldier as sensor information with intelligence collection, planning, and analysis to enhance operations and intelligence integration and provide intelligence that supports all levels of decisionmaking.

d. Protection.

(1) Future Army intelligence forces require the capability to integrate chemical, biological, radiological, nuclear, and high-yield explosives (CBRNE) and engineer sensors with intelligence collection, planning, and analysis to enhance operations and intelligence integration and provide intelligence that supports all levels of decisionmaking.

(2) Future Army intelligence forces require the capability to integrate police intelligence operations with intelligence collection, planning, and analysis to enhance operations and intelligence integration and provide intelligence that supports all levels of decisionmaking.

(3) Future Army intelligence forces require the capability to manage intelligence collection in compliance with status of forces agreements or other governing regulations to enhance operations and intelligence integration and provide intelligence that supports all levels of decisionmaking.

(4) Future Army forces require the capability to provide assistance with criminal activities intelligence with intelligence collection, planning, and analysis to enhance operations and intelligence integration and provide intelligence that supports all levels of decisionmaking.

(5) Future Army forces require the capability to provide intelligence support during security force assistance to host nation security forces to enhance operations and intelligence integration and provide intelligence that supports all levels of decisionmaking.

(6) Future Army intelligence forces require the capability to integrate every soldier as sensor information with intelligence collection, planning, and analysis to enhance operations and intelligence integration and provide intelligence that supports all levels of decisionmaking.

e. Sustainment.

(1) Future Army intelligence forces require the capability to integrate medical intelligence and surveillance operations results with intelligence collection, planning, and analysis to enhance operations and intelligence integration and provide intelligence that supports all levels of decisionmaking.

(2) Future Army intelligence forces require the capability to integrate every Soldier as sensor information with intelligence collection, planning, and analysis to enhance operations and intelligence integration and provide intelligence that supports all levels of decisionmaking.

B-5. Other warfighting function dependencies on intelligence

a. Mission command. Mission command has no dependencies of the intelligence warfighting function.

b. Movement and maneuver.

(1) Future Army maneuver forces require the capability to identify hazards, such as mines and improvised explosive devises, from standoff distances while moving to provide freedom of maneuver.

(2) Future Army maneuver forces require the capability to detect, identify, and classify threats through noncooperative methods, at ranges in excess of the threat's detection and weapon systems effective ranges, and inside the threat's detection and response time to maintain the initiative.

(3) Future Army maneuver forces require the capability to provide persistent surveillance across broad areas to understand the dynamic OE and answer CCIR.

(4) Future Army maneuver forces require the capability to conduct reconnaissance to collect precise and timely information to enable the commander to maneuver at will, to provide flexibility, and to exploit success rapidly.

(5) Future Army maneuver forces require the capability to tag, track, and locate neutral and hostile individuals in all domains to control populations.

(6) Future Army maneuver forces require cultural awareness of the AO to conduct full-spectrum operations.

(7) Future Army maneuver forces require accurate intelligence collection and analysis at company to support direct and indirect fires targeting to support the commander's maneuver scheme.

(8) Future Army maneuver forces require the capability at the company and platoon level to communicate with local populations to collect information and build partnerships.

(9) Future Army maneuver forces require aviation platforms with the capability provided by improved sensors that acquire and identify targets beyond enemy direct fire ranges and perform mine and improvised explosive device detection, in complex terrain, during joint and combined arms air-ground operations to provide lethal overmatch, early warning, and improved security for the air-ground team.

(10) Future Army maneuver forces at corps and division require the capability to monitor, collect, and analyze multiple sources of PMESII in foreign languages to determine the perceptions, attitudes, and sentiment of key populations to exert psychological influence rapidly in full-spectrum operations.

c. Fires.

(1) Future Army forces require intelligence collection and analysis capabilities to support rapid targeting and defense design to provide effective and efficient offensive and defensive fires.

(2) Future Army forces require the capability to integrate intelligence collection capabilities with fires capabilities to produce targetable data for offensive and defensive fires.

d. Protection.

(1) Future Army forces require military law enforcement to have the capability to extrapolate forensic evidence from battlefield exploitation, supporting full-spectrum operations by providing enhanced criminal intelligence to dismantle insurgent transport layers and permanently remove criminal combatants from the battlefield through the judicial process.

(2) Future Army forces require military law enforcement to have the capability to identify, investigate, document, analyze, generate, and disseminate criminal intelligence products

regarding criminals and criminal transport layers in support of kinetic targeting, judicial process, and overall force protection.

(3) Future Army forces require military law enforcement to provide the commander a more robust common operating picture (COP) as a force multiplier by leveraging military police knowledge, skills, and abilities through the development of host nation security forces, judicial processes, and community interaction.

(4) Future Army forces require military law enforcement to have the capability to support maneuver commanders as a primary advisor, trainer, and technician in the areas of forensics, criminal methodology, and law enforcement tactics, techniques, and procedures to combat threats.

(5) Future Army forces require that military law enforcement administer and maintain all criminal databases throughout all theaters of operations to maximize the application of nonclassified information and intelligence to support all judicial operations.

(6) Future Army forces require an ability to conduct site exploitation operations; to locate, search, identify, capture, and process information, materials, and personnel found on a site, analyze the collected information, and disseminate the relevant collected information and derived intelligence across all spectrums of operations.

(7) Future Army forces require that military law enforcement has the capability to collect, access, process, and exploit biometrics data to include fingerprint, handprint, iris, DNA, and facial recognition.

e. Sustainment. Sustainment has no dependencies of the intelligence warfighting function.

f. ARSOF.

(1) Future ARSOF forces require the capability to perform media exploitation.

(2) Future ARSOF forces require the capability to query biometric databases and compare on-hand biometric information to biometric information in national-level databases from the IC.

(3) Future ARSOF forces require the capability to perform field forensics and screening purposes.

(4) Future ARSOF forces require the capability to perform human terrain analysis and synthesize this information to produce products that provide a full geographic intelligence picture to the combatant commander to support full-spectrum operations.

(5) Future ARSOF forces require the capability to perform hostile force tagging, tracking, and locating.

(6) Future ARSOF forces require the capability to perform HUMINT on a larger scale, particularly concerning interrogation.

(7) Future ARSOF forces require the capability to perform signal intelligence on a larger scale.

(8) Future ARSOF forces require the capability to perform image intelligence to exploit its capabilities.

(9) Future ARSOF forces require the capability to perform measurement and signature intelligence.

(10) Future ARSOF forces require the capability to access nonorganic collection platforms and reach abilities to supporting intelligence collection managers in support of full-spectrum operations.

g. Space and high altitude.

(1) Future Army forces require the capability to provide real-time, pervasive, extended range; intertheater and intratheater global beyond line-of-sight communications relay capability and broadcast services between noncontiguous forces at the halt, at the quick halt, and on the move in all operations conditions.

(2) Future Army forces require the capability to conduct persistent imagery, MASINT, and electronic warfare support (ES) surveillance, to disseminate collected intelligence rapidly; and to reallocate and retask space and high altitude-based surveillance assets rapidly.

(3) Future Army forces require the capability to access and disseminate robust AOR COP and execution information to higher, lower, adjacent, supported, and supporting organizations.

(4) Future Army forces require the capability to provide high resolution geospatial data and comprehensive environmental information, including real-time tasking, collection, and on board or in the AOR processing, to visualize and describe the OE and assess the impact of terrain, atmosphere, weather, and high altitude variables in all operational environments and conditions.

(5) Future Army forces require the capability to provide access to a wide variety of sensors and sources simultaneously from multiple noncontiguous locations to provide timely, actionable, and relevant information in support of the planning, execution and assessment operations of the joint force and component commanders.

(6) Future Army forces require the capability to provide high altitude persistence platforms, links, and processors to enable the fusion, sharing, push, pull, and update of information from a wide variety of sensors and sources in all domains, access that information simultaneously from multiple noncontiguous locations to provide timely, actionable, and relevant information in support of the planning, execution, and assessment operations of the joint force commander and component commanders.

(7) Future Army forces require the capability to position, cue, cross-cue, task, and dynamically retask netted layers of redundant space, aerial, and surface sensors and relays.

(8) Future Army forces require the capability to provide wide area surveillance whereby multiple sensors must be able to monitor areas simultaneously to counter camouflage concealment deception operations and provide critical target information to enhance the fires planning and execution process.

h. Biometrics.

(1) Future Army forces require the capability to collect, access, process, and exploit biometrics data to include fingerprint, handprint, iris, DNA, voice and facial recognition.

(2) Future Army forces require the capability to remotely determine and detect biometric variables and parameters in all environments.

(3) Future Army forces require the capability to share, store, and reference biometrics data across multiple classified and unclassified domains.

(4) Future Army forces require the capability to nest theater and Army biometrics-enabled watch list with Under Secretary of Defense for Acquisition, Technology, and Logistics-designated DOD biometrics watch list custodian.

(5) Future Army forces require the capability to verify and correlate identities with related contextual data to enable HUMINT and CI missions.

i. Homeland defense.

(1) Future Army forces require the capability to perform intelligence collection and analysis capabilities to conduct early planning, collaboration, integration, interoperability, and information sharing to support the homeland defense and civil support missions.

(2) Future Army forces require the capability to improve intelligence interoperability and planning, training, and command and mission control requirements to support the homeland defense and civil support missions.

(3) Future Army forces require the capability to develop concepts, doctrine, systems, and infrastructure to defeat potential attacks on the U.S. homeland and to respond to defense requirements effectively, such as consequence management to support the homeland defense and civil support missions.

(4) Future Army forces require the capability to task Army elements and report analysis in a specified AO to homeland defense authority to support the homeland defense and civil support missions.

(5) Future Army forces require the capability to advise Army elements on legal requirements in a specified AO to support the homeland defense and civil support missions.

(6) Future Army forces require the capability to plan, conduct, and execute incident assessment and awareness, and intelligence, surveillance, and reconnaissance missions in the homeland in support of civil support operations.

(7) Future Army forces require the capability to conduct intelligence threat warning operations, to include the collection, analysis, and dissemination of foreign intelligence counterintelligence threat information, CI support to antiterrorism, and force protection to support the homeland defense and civil support missions.

(8) Future Army forces require the capability to establish steady-state liaison with key Federal, state, local, and tribal partners to support the homeland defense and civil support missions.

(9) Future Army forces require the capability to provide intelligence support to defense coordination officials and elements to support the homeland defense and civil support missions.

(10) Future Army forces require the capability to receive, analyze, and disseminate redacted law enforcement reporting to support force protection and intelligence trend analysis to support the homeland defense and civil support missions.

(11) Future Army forces require the capability to disseminate critical intelligence reporting to law enforcement partners to support the homeland defense and civil support missions.

(12) Future Army forces require the capability to obtain detailed weather and weather effects information and intelligence to support full-spectrum operations.

(13) Future Army forces require the capability to provide oversight for and conduct activities in accordance with intelligence oversight policy and regulations to support full-spectrum operations.

(14) Future Army forces require the capability to provide a high altitude, long loitering, persistent intelligence, surveillance, reconnaissance, and communications for rescue and humanitarian operations to support full-spectrum operations.

(15) Future Army forces require the capability to provide intelligence support for defense support of civil law enforcement agencies in accordance with DOD directives and laws to support the homeland defense and civil support missions.

(16) Future Army forces require the capability to provide intelligence support for defense critical infrastructure protection in accordance with DOD directives and laws to support the homeland defense and civil support missions.

B-6. Required capabilities to support rule of law outside the continental U.S. (OCONUS)

a. Future Army intelligence forces require the capability to provide intelligence support to the rule of law during OCONUS operations to provide the commander intelligence to support targeting and decisionmaking.

b. Future Army forces require the capability to provide intelligence support to military police intelligence operations and criminal intelligence operations.

c. Future Army forces require capability to provide CI and HUMINT liaison activities with law enforcement, host nation, and security activities.

d. Future Army forces require the capability to provide intelligence awareness and utilization of host nation-informed no strike lists when doing target development.

e. Future Army forces require the capability to provide CI and HUMINT collection that is cognizant of and practices evidence custodianship rules during CI and HUMINT collection using automated collection and analysis tools and CI and HUMINT collection peripheral sets and kits.

f. Future Army forces require the capability to manage intelligence collections to maintain compliance with status of forces agreements and/or the equivalents or other governing regulations.

g. Future Army forces require the capability to incorporate collection priorities that support shaping operations designed to bolster host nation government credibility and legitimacy.

h. Future Army forces require the capability to ensure actionable intelligence is not degraded when developing a process of allowing intelligence to be used as evidence (such as, "front load" evidentiary requirements to secure an arrest warrant).

i. Future Army forces require the capability to ensure targeting methodology remains responsive to OE operational tempo when utilizing F3EAD targeting methodology in a warrant-based operating environment.

j. Future Army forces require the capability to provide declassification of intelligence collection when envisioned, then plan for a flexible, diligent, and streamlined process with foreign disclosure officers.

k. Future Army forces require the capability to move towards transparent targeting with partnered host nation security force with parallel development of the host nation security force intelligence collection capability and parallel development of an effective CI capability to mitigate risks of infiltration.

l. Future Army forces require the capability to support development of host nation intelligence collection capabilities that are supported by the host nation's current technology and are culturally acceptable, (meaning, host nation technology may not support SIGINT, and forensics may not be culturally acceptable).

m. Future Army forces require the capability to support sensitive site exploitation (SSE) training with the partnered host nation security force.

n. Future Army forces require the capability to employ a gradual progression of integrating intelligence support to rule of law missions conducted in accordance with host nation criminal laws and procedures.

B-7. Support to IO required capabilities

a. Future Army forces require the capability to provide intelligence support to IO tasks during full-spectrum operations to provide the commander intelligence to support targeting (fires) and decisionmaking

b. Intelligence support to information tasks is the task of providing the commander information and intelligence support for targeting through nonlethal actions. It includes intelligence support to the planning and execution of mission command and control engagement, information engagement, and the individual capabilities of Army information tasks as well as assessing the effects of those operations. Key activities reflected in this task include communications, planning, synchronization, and integration of intelligence into operation plans and orders. Army intelligence supports core inform and influence activities such as electronic warfare (MI is responsible for ES, which is the search for, intercept, location, and localization of intentional or unintentional radiated electromagnetic energy), computer transport layer operations, psychological operations, military deception, and operations security.

(1) Future Army forces require the capability to identify, prioritize, and nominate IO targets.

(2) Future Army forces require the capability to integrate IO targets into the intelligence, surveillance, and reconnaissance plan.

(3) Future Army forces require the capability to conduct combat assessment on IO.

(4) Future Army forces require the capability to determine specific information requirements for IO.

(5) Future Army forces require the capability to detect and identify all aspects of threat to command, control, communications, and computer systems, to include vulnerabilities.

(6) Future Army forces require the capability to identify pertinent civil considerations that affect information engagement.

(7) Future Army forces require the capability to identify populace perceptions, sentiments, attitudes, mores, allegiances, alliances, and behaviors.

(8) Future Army forces require the capability to identify nongovernmental and international organizations in the OE.

(9) Future Army forces require the capability to identify resources and capabilities of nongovernmental and international organizations in the OE.

(10) Future Army forces require the capability to identify all relevant government agencies, organizations, or departments that affect public affairs activities.

(11) Future Army forces require the capability to identify adversary misinformation, disinformation, and propaganda capabilities.

(12) Future Army forces require the capability to identify the location, biases, and agenda of national and international media representatives in the OE.

(13) Future Army forces require the capability to identify trends reflected by the national and international media.

(14) Future Army forces require the capability to provide intelligence and information to public affairs per all applicable regulations, policies, and laws.

B-8. Support to cyber operations required capabilities

a. Future Army forces require the capability to provide intelligence support to cyber operations during full-spectrum operations, to provide the commander intelligence to support targeting (fires) and decisionmaking.

b. Information superiority enables the Army future force commander to shape the OE, but there are significant factors that affect the ability of computer network operations (CNO) to support future operations. These factors include the integration of joint, interagency, intergovernmental, and multinational information and intelligence sources, tailoring CNO capabilities to remain relevant within urban, restrictive terrain against threat forces using asymmetric tactics, tailoring CNO capabilities to collect and act on relevant information in an environment largely influenced by nongovernmental organizations, and disseminating information with greater speed.

c. Intelligence staffs and units will support cyber operations by identifying and assessing foreign intelligence threats directed towards command assets and functions. They will consider the threats to the command's information systems and transport layers as part of their overall intelligence support. This support will include but is not limited to the following required capabilities:

(1) Future Army forces require the capability to provide validated intelligence that defines the threat.

(2) Future Army forces require the capability to identify friendly actions that adversary intelligence systems and intruders observe.

(3) Future Army forces require the capability to provide intelligence requirements in support of transport layer defense.

(4) Future Army forces require the capability to identify the threat and establish policies for integrating intelligence support.

(5) Future Army forces require the capability to identify computer transport layer attack capabilities targeted against friendly mission command and information systems.

(6) Future Army forces require the capability to provide inform and influence activities and information assurance requirements in submission of CCIR.

(7) Future Army forces require the capability to conduct cyber CI investigations and technical CI operations utilizing CI and HUMINT automated collection and analysis tools.

(8) Future Army forces require the capability to provide multidiscipline counterintelligence analysis utilizing CI and HUMINT automated collection and analysis tools.

(9) Future Army forces require the capability to provide cyber CI investigations and forensics, polygraph, and technical security countermeasures utilizing CI and HUMINT collection peripheral sets and kits.

(10) Future Army forces require the capability to promulgate information systems security monitoring policy.

(11) Future Army forces require capability to access the local, regional, and national communications systems to support intelligence collection.

(12) Future Army forces require the capability to generate and feed signature data repositories.

(13) Future Army forces require the capability to conduct emitter mapping and Internet protocol network reconstruction.

B-9. Support to combating WMD required capabilities

a. Future Army intelligence forces require the capability to provide intelligence support to combating WMD during full-spectrum operations, to provide the commander intelligence to support targeting (fires) and decisionmaking.

b. Intelligence support to combating WMD. The proliferation of WMD and long-range delivery systems will enable adversaries to threaten U.S. forces at greater ranges with increased lethality and precision. These weapons are particularly appealing to developing nations and nonstate actors, such as terrorist groups, because of their relative affordability, ability to deliver massive effects, and the international political influence that results from possessing WMD. WMD could be delivered using a variety of overt and covert means, including missiles, civilian ships, or aircraft and individuals. In addition to their use as weapons of terror against civilian populations, these weapons may be employed against U.S. troop concentrations threatening our ability to project power.

c. U.S. adversaries have the potential to use modern intelligence, surveillance, and reconnaissance assets and to conduct sophisticated WMD attacks both OCONUS and in the homeland. The goal of these attacks would be to destroy key operating facilities or inflict mass casualties and create terror within and outside a given theater of operations. In addition to standard intelligence support, (that is, collections, analysis, and dissemination across all intelligence disciplines), the following required capabilities are necessary for intelligence to WMD operations to support full-spectrum operations.

(1) Future Army forces require the capability to determine threat capability to acquire or produce WMD.

(2) Future Army forces require the capability to develop WMD intelligence guidance.

(3) Future Army forces require the capability to identify threat attempts to contaminate friendly food and water supplies and infect friendly forces.

(4) Future Army forces require the capability to integrate CBRNE smart sensors with intelligence, surveillance, and reconnaissance synchronization planning.

(5) Future Army forces require the capability to integrate medical intelligence and surveillance with intelligence, surveillance, and reconnaissance synchronization planning.

(6) Future Army forces require the capability to link WMD experts with interrogators for effective exploitation of threat WMD personnel.

(7) Future Army forces require the capability to conduct scientific and technical intelligence to detect and counter WMD.

Appendix C
Intelligence Echelons

C-1. Intelligence community
Army intelligence serves as a force provider, consumer or both to several organizations in the IC. It supports military operations by providing specific intelligence products and services. Army intelligence does not normally conduct strategic intelligence operations but serves as a force provider to those efforts (that is, provision of personnel to National Security Agency, and others). However the intelligence officer and the staff (Army-brigade) must be familiar with

these organizations and the methods of obtaining information from them as necessary. These organizations are below:

a. DOD agencies include the Defense Intelligence Agency, the National Geospatial-Intelligence Agency, the National Security Agency, the Central Security Service, the National Reconnaissance Office, joint reserve intelligence centers, and other service components (Navy, Air Force, and Marines).

b. Nonmilitary members of the intelligence community include the Director of National Intelligence, the Central Intelligence Agency, the Department of State, the Department of Energy the Federal Bureau of Investigation the Department of the Treasury, the U.S. Coast Guard, the Department of Homeland Security, and the Drug Enforcement Administration.

c. Other agencies include the Department of Transportation, the Disaster Assistance Response Team within the Office of Foreign Disaster; and the U.S. Agency for International Development.

C-2. Division and above intelligence organizations

a. ASCC, corps, and division intelligence staffs. The ASCC G-2, corps G-2, and division G-2 sections provide intelligence support to each respective command and that command's subordinate units. The G-2 provides the command with information and intelligence required to generate decision superiority. Intelligence collected from organic, assigned, attached, operational control, and external sources; fused; and produced internal to the G-2 feeds the intelligence running estimate and provides the threat picture. This supports information superiority, allowing the commander to act decisively. The G-2 directs and manages intelligence activities during operations and across the noncontiguous OE.

b. ASCC intelligence organizations. Theater level MI formations provide dedicated intelligence capabilities for all intelligence disciplines to the ASCC, other Army operational level commands in the AOR, and combatant, joint, or multinational commands. They are designed to meet theater army intelligence requirements and are the foundation for ARFOR intelligence support. These units conduct sustained, regionally focused intelligence operations. While their capabilities may vary, each of these organizations serve as the focal point within the combatant command for Army intelligence requirements and can provide intelligence support to units at any echelon within the combatant command's AOR. As appropriate, personnel from these organizations may augment tactical units operating within the AOR. These organizations can be augmented by Active Army and Reserve Component.

c. Corps and division intelligence capabilities. Within each of these echelons, the intelligence capability consists of an intelligence cell that performs the following tasks:

(1) The intelligence cell requests, receives, and analyzes information from all sources to produce and distribute intelligence products. It produces intelligence on the current operation to assist the commander and staff as they monitor progress and assess the operation. It conducts continuous IPB to support future operations planning and target development. The cell develops

and tracks critical targets, performs all –source analysis, manages collection, and produces and maintains IPB products.

(2) The corps and division intelligence cells leverage the intelligence enterprise to gain access to collection assets, data, and information. These capabilities are not limited to organic or assigned Army assets, rather the cells access all available capabilities (joint, multinational, non-DOD, and others) at all echelons and locations available to them. This means that physical ownership of capabilities is not necessary in today's or tomorrows operations but rather access to capabilities is the critical factor.

d. The corps and division may require a dedicated brigade-level surveillance organization. Corps and division intelligence cells will employ this organization as well as all others assets available to them within the enterprise – intelligence and nonintelligence.

C-3. Army intelligence capabilities brigade and below

a. Intelligence capabilities within the BCT remain a critical component of the Army intelligence enterprise. However, its primary mission must remain the provision of timely intelligence to the BCT commander by developing situational awareness of the enemy, terrain, and weather, and civil considerations and synchronizing intelligence collection activities with the intelligence, surveillance, and reconnaissance integration effort. The BCT S-2 uses available capabilities to provide intelligence products and recommendations to the BCT commander supporting the brigade's execution of operations. Intelligence, surveillance, and reconnaissance activities focus on the requirement to answer the CCIRs and satisfy PIRs.

b. The BCT must possess the capability to provide the brigade commander and his staff as well as subordinate commands with collection, analysis, and dissemination of intelligence information and products. Co-creation of context and the requisite enhanced fusion of operations and intelligence must provide continuous refinement to the COP. MI Soldiers must synchronize all intelligence (and available nonintelligence) capabilities (organic and external to the BCT), as directed by the BCT S-3 and S-2X.

Appendix D
ARSOF Intelligence

D-1. Introduction

a. ARSOF is an integral part of the Army and the joint force and provides the nation with unique, sophisticated, and tailored capabilities. ARSOF Soldiers are specially selected, trained, and equipped, and possess unique individual and collective capabilities that connect U.S. Government intent and actions to operational and strategic effects. ARSOF is able to achieve strategic effects through tactical and operational success because it operates in a joint, interagency, and combined environment as a matter of course, and it brings Soldiers who are trained and educated to solve, or assist in solving, complex political-military challenges and to operate in ambiguous and high-risk environments. However, ARSOF rarely succeeds when operating unilaterally and at critical times requires intelligence enabler support.

b. The U.S. Army Special Operations Command (USASOC), the Army component of the joint U.S. Special Operations Command, is among the most diverse organizations in the U.S. military, bringing a broad range of competencies and disciplines to support geographic combatant commanders (GCC) and ambassadors worldwide. The fundamental mission of USASOC is two-fold: to organize, train, and equip ARSOF units and Soldiers; and to deploy them worldwide to meet the requirements of war plans, the GCCs' theater security cooperation plan, and ambassadors' mission strategic plans. USASOC when exercising its Title 10 responsibilities, recruits, assesses, selects, organizes, trains, equips, and provides forces and capabilities along three lines of effort - investment in people, persistent engagement, and operations. These lines provide the framework to prepare ARSOF Soldiers and units for deployment and provide to GCCs and ambassadors around the world, options for countering the full spectrum of threats.

c. Soldiers with these skills are in high demand across the Army, meaning Army shortages translate into ARSOF shortages. One of the critical enablers is the full range of intelligence, surveillance, and reconnaissance capabilities. Along with ARSOF, all military forces have benefited from the increase in intelligence, surveillance, and reconnaissance capabilities, most notably the use of UAS.

d. However, platforms alone are not sufficient. To be effective, information obtained from the "unblinking eye" must be processed, exploited, and disseminated, which requires intelligence analysts and communications systems (that is, a dedicated, multidiscipline, all-source intelligence effort), including sufficient bandwidth, to disseminate the intelligence. The ability to fuse, assess, and analyze information and disseminate it to the right organization in a timely manner has allowed ARSOF and general purpose forces to capture or kill high value targets; it is the intelligence capability that underpins successful operations around the world.

D-2. Intelligence structure

a. The ARSOF intelligence structure will promote cooperation and operational integration of ARSOF intelligence activities with its joint, interagency, intergovernmental, and multinational partners. ARSOF's core activities directly support the irregular warfare operational environment, as well as the full spectrum of conflict required to overcome a combination of hybrid threats and adaptive adversaries in complex operating environments.

b. To operate effectively under conditions of uncertainty and complexity in an era of persistent conflict, future ARSOF and leaders must strive to reduce uncertainty through understanding the situation in depth, developing the situation through action, fighting for information, and continually reassessing emerging situations. Effective application of intelligence design can reduce uncertainty. However, ARSOF commanders will still have to make decisions with partial, inaccurate, or contradictory information. Accomplishing challenging intelligence missions and responding to a broad range of threats and population-centric factors will require ARSOF intelligence capabilities that have a high degree of operational adaptability and flexibility.

c. The demands for future ARSOF intelligence requirements and capabilities will continue to evolve as the U.S. navigates in a world of persistent conflict. ARSOF intelligence must be proactive with technological innovation and acquisition. The U.S. military technical, organizational, and doctrinal advances will bring both improved capabilities and increased complexity. Economic, political, diplomatic, and social factors will influence tactical and operational actions to a far greater extent, all the way to the smallest unit level.

d. ARSOF distributed and simultaneous operations demand the right knowledge at the right time, and comprehension of more aspects and surface area in the operational environment. Difficult environments and adaptive enemy operations dictate highly granular intelligence. Large amounts of intelligence and other types of information demand rapid and accurate processing, analysis, and distribution capacity. Knowledge management and education of information and intelligence consumers that feed military decisionmaking cycles are keys to future ARSOF success in the operating environment. ARSOF intelligence assets must be highly adaptive and aggressively seek fusion and integration with the joint, Army, interagency, international, and multinational communities to meet the intelligence demands for 2016-2028.

D-3. Military problem and intelligence

a. Shared understanding. Complexity is an enduring characteristic of preparation of the environment shaping activities through combat operations. ARSOF decisions made by lower echelons normally have strategic implications and must be made with an appropriate understanding of the strategic context. ARSOF intelligence operations and activities must enhance this shared understanding vertically, horizontally, across, and through the joint battle space as ARSOF conducts small unit, distributed operations through campaigns planned and conducted by the joint special operations task force (JSOTF) and/or the theater special operations command (TSOC).

b. Intelligence and operational knowledge management. Developing and applying disciplined constructs and tools to frame problems, aid campaign design, and support the commander's decision cycle is crucial. ARSOF requires further evolutionary development of an integrated intelligence and knowledge management enterprise. This enterprise approach of technology, people, and processes must be capable of processing, exploiting (analyzing), and disseminating anticipatory predictive, time sensitive information and intelligence up, down, and laterally. Current intelligence analysts use as many as five intelligence systems simultaneously to meet current intelligence and knowledge management requirements for JSOTFs and TSOCs.

c. Additionally, deployed intelligence elements have limited analyst overwatch or reachback for analysis of complex problems. The deployed analyst requires an intelligence and knowledge management enterprise that gives the analyst access to analytical support for areas in which the analyst lacks expertise (such as, cultural or social sciences) or to provide additional analytical capability when the analyst lacks the time to produce all the products the commander requires.

d. Professionalizing the ARSOF intelligence operator. The ARSOF intelligence structure has a two-fold mission to support both direct and indirect activities, particularly as they relate to irregular warfare. This requires planners, collection managers, collectors, and analysts capable of going beyond the six primary core military intelligence tasks (protection, situation development, target development, indications and warning, intelligence, and battle damage assessment). ARSOF intelligence operators, not only must be masters of F3EAD, but must also be well versed on the psychological, cultural, political, and human dimensions of warfare. The ability to provide the commander information and intelligence to influence credibly relevant populations and nongovernmental centers of power is essential to ARSOF future success. Current ARSOF military intelligence practitioners come with entry-level knowledge (taught at the Intelligence Center of Excellence, Fort Huachuca, Arizona) and with varying degrees of operational experience. Consequently there is great variation in the skill level and capabilities among individual intelligence operators.

D-4. ARSOF lines of effort

a. Persistent engagement. Persistent engagement is a line of effort which supports all elements of national power and defense, development, and diplomacy to prevent conflicts and enable friends, partners, and allies to defend their sovereignty and eliminate ungoverned and undergoverned spaces where irregular threats seek sanctuary. ARSOF conducts special operations to prepare or shape the environment prior to crisis. Two primary special operations forces (SOF) core activities are foreign internal defense and security force assistance. These core activities contribute directly to support theater engagement plans and theater security cooperation plans. The ARSOF intelligence structure must continue to focus operations, activities, and analysis on a populace-centric approach while developing long term, regional, and country experts capable of drilling down to specific joint special operations areas within priority countries.

b. Operations. ARSOF operations are logically divided into two approaches, direct and indirect. These efforts are applied directly against the enemy or as actions applied indirectly to influence the operational environment, more specifically towards the populace. ARSOF intelligence must continue to improve its agility through scalable intelligence slices to support a special forces operational detachment. ARSOF operational challenges include employing intelligence enterprise-like functions with very limited architecture, IO systems, and bandwidth to support small footprint operations.

c. Investment, people with purpose. ARSOF must develop predeployment blocks of irregular warfare, specific joint intelligence functional training that focuses on applying core intelligence tradecraft skills to regional problems and scenarios in each combatant commander's AOR using the latest commander's concept of operations, tactics, techniques, and procedures, and battle rhythms. ARSOF must provide recommended irregular warfare related elective courses and training for intelligence personnel across ARSOF to improve knowledge of special capabilities. This training should include courses such as: counterterrorism network analysis, threat finance, IO, cyber warfare, use of hostile force tagging, tracking, and locating technologies, unattended sensors, ground SIGINT teams for target development and close in targeting, biometrics and SSE, document and media exploitation (DOMEX) as well as PMESII-PT.

d. In terms of education, ARSOF intelligence operators must attend advanced joint, Army, SOF, and intelligence community courses. In addition to mandatory HQ USASOC introductory and the Defense Intelligence Agency dynamic situation assessment and prediction courses, civilian and military analysts will be required to select and take courses on ARSOF. Courses may include ARSOF organization, missions, and planning; Joint Special Operations University's basic and advanced irregular warfare courses, Air Force's Special Operations School cross cultural communications and regional orientation classes; foreign disclosure officer accreditation, intelligence planning, joint intelligence preparation of the OE courses, and the asymmetrical irregular warfare intelligence courses offered by Joint Military Intelligence Training Center.

D-5. ARSOF intelligence required capabilities and dependencies

a. Future Army forces require the capability to develop and maintain shared situational awareness and understanding which includes the ability to access a COP and present current and/or forecast information on adversary and friendly forces, neutral elements, the environment and geospatial information to support full-spectrum operations.

b. Future Army forces require the capability to manage knowledge, the systematic process of discovering, selecting, organizing, distilling, sharing, developing, and using information in a social domain context, to improve ARSOF's effectiveness in support of full-spectrum operations.

c. Future Army forces require the capability to conduct intelligence, surveillance, and reconnaissance planning and direction which includes the ability to develop intelligence requirements, coordinate and position the appropriate collection assets, from the national to the tactical level, to ensure robust situational awareness and knowledge of intended domains, to support full-spectrum operations.

d. Future Army forces require advanced collection capabilities in sufficient numbers and with the flexibility to adapt to the future operating environment and the enemy's signatures, to acquire precise and timely information to support full-spectrum operations.

e. Future Army forces require integrated knowledge of the theater environment, such as terrain, weather, infrastructure, culture, demographics, and neutral entities to understand the environment better in support of full-spectrum operations.

f. Future Army forces require the capability at all echelons to conduct analysis of PMESII-PT aspects of the AO to allow commanders at all levels the ability to deal with all aspects of their operational responsibilities, in support of full-spectrum operations.

g. Future Army forces require the capability to process and transform data and information rapidly and accurately into usable knowledge across a wide range of subjects from military sustainment to culture and economics in support of full-spectrum operations.

h. Future Army forces require the capability to disseminate an overall picture of the adversary and the OE while supporting core special operations tasks across the full spectrum of conflict at all echelons in support of full-spectrum operations.

i. Future Army forces require the capability to detect, identify, locate, and maintain persistent surveillance of WMD, objects, and events to conduct ARSOF core tasks counter proliferation of WMD and counterterrorism.

j. Future Army forces require the capability to detect, identify, and locate terrorist personnel, objects, and events to conduct counterterrorism, as well as support other irregular warfare activities in support of full-spectrum operations.

Appendix E
Homeland Defense and Civil Support Intelligence

E-1. Introduction
Future Army intelligence forces require a capability to support, plan, coordinate, and deconflict intelligence operations in support of homeland defense and civil support operations.

E-2. Background

a. Decision point 36 established an ASCC U.S. Army Forces North (USARNORTH) as the ASCC for the U.S. Northern Command (USNORTHCOM). Realignment of USNORTHCOM and operations with AOR, dated 25 February 2008, established USARNORTH as the standing joint force land component command (JFLCC) for USNORTHCOM with operational control of Joint Task Force-Civil Support and Joint Task Force-North. USARNORTH has two major general-level contingency command posts that serve as command and control HQ during major contingency operations within the AOR. The Unified Command Plan, dated 17 December 2008, extended the USNORTHCOM AOR, and subsequently, the USARNORTH AOR to include Canada, Mexico, the Bahamas, Turks and Caicos Islands, and the U.S. Virgin Islands.

b. USARNORTH mission statement. USARNORTH, the JFLCC, and the ASCC to USNORTHCOM conducts homeland defense, civil support operations, and theater security cooperation activities to protect America and its way of life.

c. The USARNORTH G2 mission statement. Meet the combatant commander's daily operational requirements by providing predictive and actionable foreign intelligence and counterintelligence, threat estimates, and timely warning of worldwide threats targeting the USARNORTH AOR using fused all-source intelligence to support homeland defense, regional terrorism missions, defense support to civil authorities (DSCA) operations, and theater security cooperation; respond to command, subordinate, and component PIRs and CCIRs; coordinate the joint intelligence activities of participating commands; support two standing task forces and two contingency command posts; leverage support from USNORTHCOM and national level intelligence agencies; and, as appropriate, share intelligence and information with Federal, state, and local intelligence, law enforcement, and emergency management agencies.

d. The USARNORTH JFLCC AOR includes the U.S. (the 48 contiguous states, the District of Columbia and Alaska), Canada, Mexico, U.S. Virgin Islands, Puerto Rico, British Virgin Islands, Bermuda, Bahamas, Turks and Caicos Islands, and St. Pierre and Miquelon. The JFLCC area of interest includes the entire world. Operations throughout the world affect the projection of forces that reside in the USARNORTH AOR. The operation of transnational terrorist organizations and other hostile elements around the world affect the JFLCC AOR as well.

e. USARNORTH's top priority is homeland defense and civil support missions, as directed by USNORTHCOM. When directed by USNORTHCOM, USARNORTH fulfills its DSCA mission by responding to requests for assistance in accordance with the USNORTHCOM Executive Order, the national response framework, and DOD policies and guidance.

f. The national response framework coordinating framework for support is provided under the Disaster Relief and Emergency Assistance Act. The Stafford Act and the Economy Act are the major pieces of legislation that govern the Federal response. Support under these laws ranges from small-scale efforts to large-scale operations involving thousands of DOD personnel. This plan covers the spectrum of DSCA operations and supporting intelligence tasks to USNORTHCOM and USARNORTH, and USARNORTH's subordinate standing joint task forces.

g. The Joint Strategic Capabilities Plan 2008 sets forth DSCA planning requirements for the commander of USNORTHCOM that include preparation of an all-hazards plan to support civil authorities, including those hazards defined by the national planning scenarios.

h. USARNORTH has 11 defense coordinating officers and/or defense coordinating elements assigned to the Federal Emergency Management Association regions to assist civil authorities in planning, coordinating, and executing DSCA for contingency operations and consequence management. Such critical activities necessitate a significant standing intelligence requirement.

i. The commander of USNORTHCOM, has designated USARNORTH as the national lead for military-to-military land component engagement with the Mexican army and air force.

j. Intelligence requirements for the continental U.S. (CONUS) JFLCC derived from higher HQ are below:

(1) USARNORTH must develop and disseminate antiterrorism and force protection intelligence products to support the Installation Management Command and the Army Material Command.

(2) Provide administrative support for Army forces assigned to USNORTHCOM in response to homeland defense or civil support operations.

(3) Training, readiness, and oversight of the CBRNE consequence management reaction force.

(4) As the standing JFLCC, maintain lead operational authority for CBRNE consequence management and counterdrug and counternarcotics terrorism in the USNORTHCOM AOR.

(5) Develop and provide base support installation recommendations with other service components to USNORTHCOM J3 during operations.

(6) Coordinate national logistics staging areas requests and recommendations with USNORTHCOM J3. On order, conduct joint reception, staging onward movement, and integration operations in support of DOD forces conducting USNORTHCOM operations within the USNORTHCOM AOR. Provide ASCC operational planning and execution support for Army forces to support North American Aerospace Defense Command operations. Conduct the USNORTHCOM antiterrorism program and force protection responsibilities for all Army personnel in the USNORTHCOM AOR. Provide training and external evaluations for the National Guard WMD civil support teams, and conduct the DSCA course.

k. Through theater security cooperation, attend the annual border commander's conference, and enhance information sharing for counterdrug operations.

l. As the JFLCC (Mexican army and air force), Joint Task Force-North efforts enhance cooperation with the Mexican Army. In Mexican military regions, border disasters have enhanced cooperation at the operational level. Enhanced cooperation leads to potential training assistance and training opportunities. The JFLCC also assumes land forces Canada cross border movement approval authority and enforces the bilateral U.S.-Canada civil assistance plan. Finally, the JFLCC assumes administrative control of the Army personnel exchange program.

E-3. Operational environment

a. USARNORTH operates in a changing and uncertain security environment. A range of threats, in all domains, represents an immediate and future challenge for the command. Whereas the enemies of yesterday were relatively predictable, homogeneous, hierarchical, and resistant to change, current adversaries include those who are unpredictable, diverse, thoroughly networked, and dynamic. These adversaries benefit from technologies and materials readily accessible in world markets, including disruptive systems and the ingredients required to fabricate WMD. USARNORTH shares the fundamental responsibility of defending the U.S. homeland as well as the broader USARNORTH AOR from external threats. Homeland defense is USARNORTH's top priority in support of the national goal of securing the U.S. from direct attack through an active defense.

b. In addition to its primary role, USARNORTH must also be prepared to provide DSCA and support to U.S. civil authorities (Federal, state, local, and tribal) by responding to natural and manmade disasters. Natural disasters, such as hurricanes, earthquakes, or pandemics, can exceed the capabilities of civilian responders, and thus require significant allocation of military resources to help mitigate their effects and to support relief and recovery efforts. Likewise, a terrorist attack, particularly one involving WMD, can cause catastrophic losses requiring substantial civil support and DSCA.

c. North America is comprised of three important U.S. neighbors, Canada, Mexico, and the Commonwealth of the Bahamas, who share many compatible national characteristics, including open and intertwined economies. From a security perspective, the huge flow of goods and people, combined with economic and structural asymmetries between Canada, the U.S., and Mexico, creates security issues unlike those found anywhere else in the world. The geographically dispersed island nations of the Caribbean, and specifically the Commonwealth of the Bahamas, create unique challenges within USARNORTH AOR. While the U.S. maintains a broad array of active defense and security related agreements with Canada, the absence of any such agreement with Mexico may hinder coordinated efforts towards combating transnational threats such as drug trafficking organizations as well as potential WMD threats and incidents.

d. The JFLCC AOR includes the U.S. (the 48 contiguous states, the District of Columbia, and Alaska), Canada, Mexico, U.S. Virgin Islands, Puerto Rico, British Virgin Islands, Bermuda, Bahamas, Turks and Caicos Islands, and St. Pierre and Miquelon. The JFLCC area of interest includes the whole world. The operations of transnational terrorist organizations and other hostile elements around the world affect the JFLCC AOR operations and the projection of DOD forces that reside in the USARNORTH AOR.

e. The specific intelligence requirements from higher HQ include the following:

(1) Conduct 24x7 intelligence threat warning operations with sensitive compartmented information capability.

(2) Maintain the ability to tailor and apply strategic, operational, and tactical level intelligence analysis to support DOD and interagency operations.

(3) Develop CCIR, PIRs, and requests for information in support of assigned missions.

(4) Execute intelligence planning functions in support of assigned missions.

(5) Conduct intelligence liaison with interagency partners (for example, intelligence, law enforcement agencies, and emergency management).

(6) Conduct mission in accordance with intelligence oversight.

(7) Maintain a capability to plan and conduct incident assessment and awareness, and intelligence, surveillance, and reconnaissance.

(8) Maintain multidiscipline collection requirements capability to support operations.

(9) Collect and share operational information.

(10) Along with the JFACC, incorporate and synchronize intelligence-related activities with operational collection requirements and provide continuous feedback to ensure optimum utilization of high demand, low density airborne incident assessment and awareness, and intelligence, surveillance, and reconnaissance assets.

(11) Produce operational intelligence and prepare intelligence products.

(12) Complete intelligence estimates and reports as required.

(13) Provide input to critical infrastructure program inspection reports to meet USNORTHCOM and DA requirements.

(14) Execute theater intelligence collection management for the land component.

(15) Execute theater request for information management for the land component.

(16) Maintain a 24/7/365 intelligence watch to perform indications, warning, and situational awareness for the land component.

(17) Maintain all-source intelligence support elements to provide multidiscipline intelligence and CI support to JFLCC, standing joint task forces, and contingency command posts.

(18) Provide intelligence oversight and other intelligence related staff oversight of subordinate units and joint task forces.

(19) Support USNORTHCOM intelligence related theater security cooperation efforts.

(20) Ensure incident assessment and awareness, and intelligence, surveillance, and reconnaissance activities are conducted in strict compliance with the U.S. Constitution and applicable laws.

(21) Coordinate and deconflict CI and HUMINT.

(22) Support intelligence to planning, operations, exercises, and special events.

(23) Provide intelligence geospatial support.

(24) Develop modified threat vulnerability assessment.

(25) Evaluate intelligence products.

(26) Develop threat link analysis products.

E-4. Integrated theater Army intelligence enterprise mission

The theater Army intelligence cells are responsible for the synchronization and integration of intelligence operations throughout the USARNORTH AOR. Sections and elements of the cells are either embedded in or coordinated with integrating staff elements to facilitate synchronization. The intelligence cell depends on the tactical intelligence battalion and aligned Army Reserve component units for intelligence collection, single source analysis, and all source fusion to meet the Theater Army's intelligence needs, and builds durable intelligence partnerships and partner intelligence capability and capacity, through military-to-military, training, and exercise engagements.

E-5. Concept of operations

a. NORTHCOM has combatant command authority over all assigned and attached forces provided to it. USARNORTH is the JFLCC for NORTHCOM. The JFLCC includes the theater Army commander, the theater Army HQ, and all Army organizations and units, personnel, and installations assigned or attached to the combatant command.

b. The JFLCC-J2 is the land component focal point for intelligence and is responsible for coordination between the JFLCC J2, outside agencies, and subordinate intelligence activities required to support the combatant commander's daily operational requirements. The JFLCC defines the intelligence requirements for the land component, prioritizes subordinate land forces requirements, and provides representation for the land component and its subordinates at the joint force commander's daily joint targeting and coordination board. Pertinent intelligence oversight, appropriate DOD regulations, and proper use of procedures govern all JFLCC intelligence operations.

c. The JLFCC J2 staff incorporates and synchronizes all incident assessment and awareness, and intelligence, surveillance, and reconnaissance operations including HUMINT and CI operations with NORTHCOM J2X staff. The JFLCC J2 will conduct incident assessment and awareness, and intelligence, surveillance, and reconnaissance operations in accordance with USNORTHCOM, Joint Intelligence Operations Center-North, incident assessment and awareness, and intelligence, surveillance, and reconnaissance concepts of operation. The JFLCC states operational requirements and provides continuous feedback to ensure optimum incident assessment and awareness, and intelligence, surveillance, and reconnaissance support to operations. Consistent with the Federal Bureau of Investigation authority within the IC for collecting foreign intelligence and counterintelligence within CONUS, neither JFLCC J2 nor subordinate DOD forces will engage in domestic intelligence activities while operating within the joint operations area without specific approval from the Secretary of Defense.

(1) USARNORTH is an operational HQ and must maintain warfighting capabilities for any short duration crises. USARNORTH intelligence capabilities support Phase 0 (shape), Phase 1 (anticipate), Phase 2 (respond), limited Phase 3 (operate), Phase 4 (stabilize), and Phase 5

(transition). USARNORTH provides a regionally-oriented, long-term Army presence for military engagement, security cooperation and deterrence, and provides support to joint and Army forces operating in a joint operations area opened within the NORTHCOM AOR. Army operational-level organizations assigned to the theater Army provide theater-level capabilities necessary to perform operational-level tasks as well as to assist and augment subordinate tactical organizations.

(2) USARNORTH intelligence operations are inherently joint and interagency. USARNORTH must be able to develop contacts, understand, and work with other U.S. government agencies, international governments and agencies, intergovernmental organizations, nongovernmental organizations, and private companies. These activities require extensive intelligence liaison and interagency coordination to build working relationships that complement activities. This interdependence and complexity extends beyond traditional DOD capabilities.

(3) USARNORTH must conduct recurring and progressive theater security cooperation operations, including military-to-military engagements, institutional support, key leader visits, and multinational joint operations. As a result, the ARNORTH intelligence enterprise must be able to plan, prepare, collect, process, analyze, produce, disseminate, exploit, and assess intelligence from a vast array of sources, cultures, and languages to support counterterrorism operations, counter-trafficking operations, and peace support operations. However, the theater Army intelligence cell is only structured to conduct limited planning, preparation, production, dissemination, and assessment. It is totally dependent upon its organic capabilities and the combatant commander, Joint Intelligence Operations Center, to conduct intelligence preparation of the operational environment, collection planning and management, collection, processing, analysis and in-depth assessment.

E-6. Required capabilities

a. Future Army forces require the ability to conduct early planning, collaboration, integration, interoperability, and information sharing in support of homeland defense and civil support.

b. Future Army forces require the capability to improve intelligence interoperability and planning, training, and command and mission control requirements for homeland defense operations; accomplished through collaborative venues such as exercises, development of systems with mutually beneficial capabilities, conferences, and workshops that build integration, interoperability, and provide access to military intelligence training courses.

c. Future Army forces require the capability to advise Army elements on legal requirements in a specified AO in support of homeland defense and civil support.

d. Future Army forces require the capability to plan, conduct, and execute incident assessment and awareness and intelligence, surveillance, and reconnaissance missions in the homeland in support of civil support operations.

e. Future Army forces require the capability to conduct intelligence threat warning operations, to include the collection, analysis, and dissemination of foreign intelligence and counterintelligence threat information, to include CI support to antiterrorism and force protection in support of homeland defense.

f. Future Army forces require the capability to establish liaison with key Federal, state, local, and tribal partners in support of homeland defense and civil support.

g. Future Army forces require the capability to provide intelligence support to defense coordination officials and elements in support of homeland defense and civil support.

h. Future Army forces require the capability to receive, analyze, and disseminate redacted law enforcement reporting to support force protection and intelligence trend analysis in support of homeland defense and civil support.

i. Future Army forces require the capability to disseminate critical intelligence reporting to law enforcement partners in support of homeland defense and civil support.

j. Future Army forces require the capability to provide a high altitude, long loitering, persistent intelligence, surveillance, and reconnaissance and communications for rescue and humanitarian operations in support of homeland defense and civil support.

k. Future Army forces require the capability to provide intelligence support in the homeland for defense support of civil law enforcement agencies in accordance with DOD directives and laws, in support of homeland defense and civil support.

l. Future Army forces require the capability to provide intelligence support in the homeland for defense critical infrastructure protection in accordance with DOD directives and laws, in support of homeland defense and civil support.

Appendix F
Intelligence Future DOTMLPF Considerations

F-1. Introduction

a. Military intelligence must be able to provide a force that can be tailored to commanders' demands arising from different operational environments and different missions embraced by full-spectrum operations. The requirements determination process must be refined to provide capability developers and providers a better understanding of intelligence needs in specific OE-mission contexts. Adoption of an improved requirements process—plus better execution— would be expected to result in, for example, an institutional appreciation of the fact that even in an irregular warfare context, the intelligence needs just at the BCT echelon might be significantly different for a BCT engaged in stability operations than a BCT engaged in high value target tracking and targeting. In the former, a premium might be placed on the need for capability to help gain an in-depth understanding of the population whereas the latter high value target might instead place a premium on precision target location.

b. Expected OE and mission changes, however, make it unrealistic to field a one-size-fits-all-circumstances MI force and suggests strongly that the MI force, if it is to be truly adaptable, must have built in the means to adapt to such varying operational demands. MI force flexibility will be required not just at the BCT but at every echelon. For this notion to become reality, it will require several critical enablers that build upon an improved, fine-grained understanding of requirements.

(1) First, the Army must come to a consensus about MI's core competencies. The MI proponent, in coordination with the proponents of other supported warfighting functions, must determine what constitutes the support expected from the MI force in operational situations and the support that has linkage to the intelligence warfighting function but might be performed by non-MI forces.

(2) Second, the MI proponent must decide how it will build the operational MI force in a way that will support its ability to flexibly tailor and deliver the right capability to supported commanders, independent of echelon, operational theme, OE, or mission.

(3) Third, the MI proponent must lead the effort to identify and resolve all issues associated with providing such routine, tailored MI support to future Army forces.

(4) Fourth, although it is critical for the proponent to identify and resolve systemic issues that might limit or impede effective tailored support to the operating force, it is no less important for supported and MI commanders in the operating force to understand how to employ the MI force end-to-end under actual OE-mission conditions. To this end, leader development and training must lay the necessary ground to permit each commander to effectively tailor and employ MI forces under realistic and changing operational conditions.

(5) Fifth, some MI skills are years in the making. As such, proficiency demands that MI forces remain fully engaged in real and realistic work and training; exposure to real operational intelligence challenges cannot be limited to just those periods when intelligence forces are deployed. This challenge has always confronted intelligence; however, with less-structured, harder to understand threats and adversaries, it is even more imperative that the Army confront the challenge of how to keep its intelligence force engaged and trained all the time. The training challenges will likely call for tighter, stronger relationships between the operating and generating forces. The nature of these relationships may cause us to confront cultural differences in perspectives and practical challenges in execution. However, without a viable partnership of all stakeholders with interest in maintaining a proficient MI force, institutional training will be misaligned, uncoordinated, or unsupportive of the operating forces' demands for a high-performing, capable intelligence force.

c. Outlined below are DOTMLPF and homeland defense considerations for army combat developers, trainers, and human resource professionals use in execution of the capabilities-based assessment. These broadly stated considerations are a start point for analysis that should be modified or added to based on future emerging lessons learned. Use of these considerations will aid the development of persistent global intelligence operations in the future OE. These considerations will facilitate an evolutionary process of integrated intelligence and operational changes required to develop a tailored MI force package that can be flexibly provided to commanders across the range of anticipated operating environments and mission sets.

F-2. Doctrine

a. Doctrinal publications from all schools and centers of excellence require review and update to reflect implementation of future intelligence concept initiatives. Intelligence doctrine must pursue initiatives to increase its effectiveness.

b. Use network to provide timely distribution of FMs, tactics, techniques, and procedures, and training circulars.

c. Use Wiki software to interlink doctrinal writers and field users via web technology to facilitate exchange of lessons learned and doctrinal development.

d. Develop and implement a tactical and operational intelligence taxonomy that delineates the general and special relationships of the given OE, adversary, technology, cultural, or social system.

F-3. Organizational

a. Army intelligence should make organizational changes to establish and expand capabilities and capacity in the following areas:

(1) Design tailored MI force packages that can be flexibly provided to commanders across the range of anticipated operating environments and mission sets.

(2) Develop an MI force that is deployment ready.

(3) Develop policy, procedure, and force design that supports tailored force capability flow.

(4) Develop an MI force that is joint-leveraging, integrated with whole of government organizations and coalitions on mission- and OE-specific bases.

(5) Develop an MI force that makes efficient and effective use of each component.

b. HUMINT (interrogations). Future Army forces require interrogation organizational capacity at the tactical, operational, and strategic levels. Each echelon will exploit and reinforce its success with other interrogations elements or teams and advanced source operations teams at the BCT, division, and corps levels.

(1) HUMINT (military source operations (MSO)). MSO focuses on exploiting contacts and source transport layers identified through key leader engagements conducted and others as designated by the unit commander. HUMINT personnel conduct MSO in support of the maneuver element. These operations are designed to collect intelligence related to force protection and unit level mission support. They are also responsible for spotting and assessing

potential sources that respond to multiple echelon requirements (such as, BCT, division, and corps).

(2) DOMEX. As an integral part of the OE, DOMEX is an increasingly specialized full-time mission requiring advanced automation and communications support, analytical support, and expert linguists. DOMEX and translation operations were once considered purely HUMINT processing activities directly associated with language capabilities and extensive background knowledge in area studies. Current doctrinal thought acknowledges that HUMINT is no longer the sole asset capable of conducting DOMEX operations. Personnel involved in DOMEX do not require HUMINT training to screen or translate a document, particularly since the unit may better utilize its HUMINT assets to conduct the HUMINT mission. DOMEX is an Armywide responsibility and while HUMINT assets may be utilized to perform the DOMEX mission when available, HUMINT is a consumer of DOMEX information, rather than the major provider.

(3) Analytic capabilities. The emerging lesson learned from OEF and OIF operations is the need for CoISTs in future operations. The CoIST effort adds an analytical capability to address increasing demand for analytic support at the maneuver battalion and maneuver company level

(4) Battlefield surveillance brigade and MI battalion modifications. Based on lessons learned in OEF and OIF operations, and OCONUS operations, current SIGINT operations are needed to add a cryptologic support and SIGINT terminal guidance capability to address the increasing complexity and criticality of SIGINT operations.

(5) MI brigade modifications. Theater level intelligence structure will be tailored to suit the missions of the respective ASCC and combatant commanders they support. In general, each theater echelon intelligence organization should contain the following capabilities: All-source fusion, operations, plans, and watch, CI, SIGINT, MASINT, GEOINT, satellite communications, common ground station, intelligence, and electronic warfare maintenance. These organizations will be capable of addressing Phase 0 (shape), and Phase 1 (anticipate), Phase 2 (respond), Phase 3 (operate), and Phase 4 (stabilize) theater requirements or homeland defense and civil support as required.

(6) Tactical overwatch. The Army strategy envisions deliberate use of the entire Army MI force through various enterprises, which would provide cohesive, tailored, and sustained intelligence support to the training, readiness, and deployment cycles of corps, divisions, and brigades. The Army will conduct tactical overwatch from home station locations for additional reachback and tactical overwatch or regional support capabilities.

(7) Ensure that tables of organization and equipment and modified tables of organization and equipment at all echelons are prepared to support assigned Air Force weather teams (in accordance with the most current Air Force Wartime Manpower Study.

c. Formation and modification of Army analysis sections and organizations: Army intelligence not only requires innovative analyst training but also more adaptable and flexible analytic organizational structure. Formation of Army analytical sections and organizations require increased consideration in their construction and use. The following are items to consider in this effort:

(1) Will the analyst's unit perform current operations, long range analysis, or will it be required to do both?

(2) Will the analyst's unit be focused on a specific geographic unit or will it have split focus between multiple geographic units? If so, how many geographic units can be covered and still maintain continuity?

(3) What virtual extensions will the analyst's unit require to other national, joint, Army, host nation, and coalition analyst units for analytic integration?

(4) What are the processes for analyst to commander and leader exchanges?

(5) What are the processes for analyst to collection managers and collectors for the purposes of collector selection and source validation?

(6) What are the processes to allow analysts to impact collection?

(7) What is the right mix of forward and reachback analytical and exploitation capabilities?

d. The joint MI college publication[8] identifies a set of desired analyst characteristic, abilities, knowledge, and skills. While not every candidate will possess every item, the lists are a good start for developing an assessment instrument for future Army analysts (see figure F-1 below).

e. Analysts must absorb information with the thoroughness of historians, organize it with the skill of librarians, and disseminate it with the zeal of journalists.

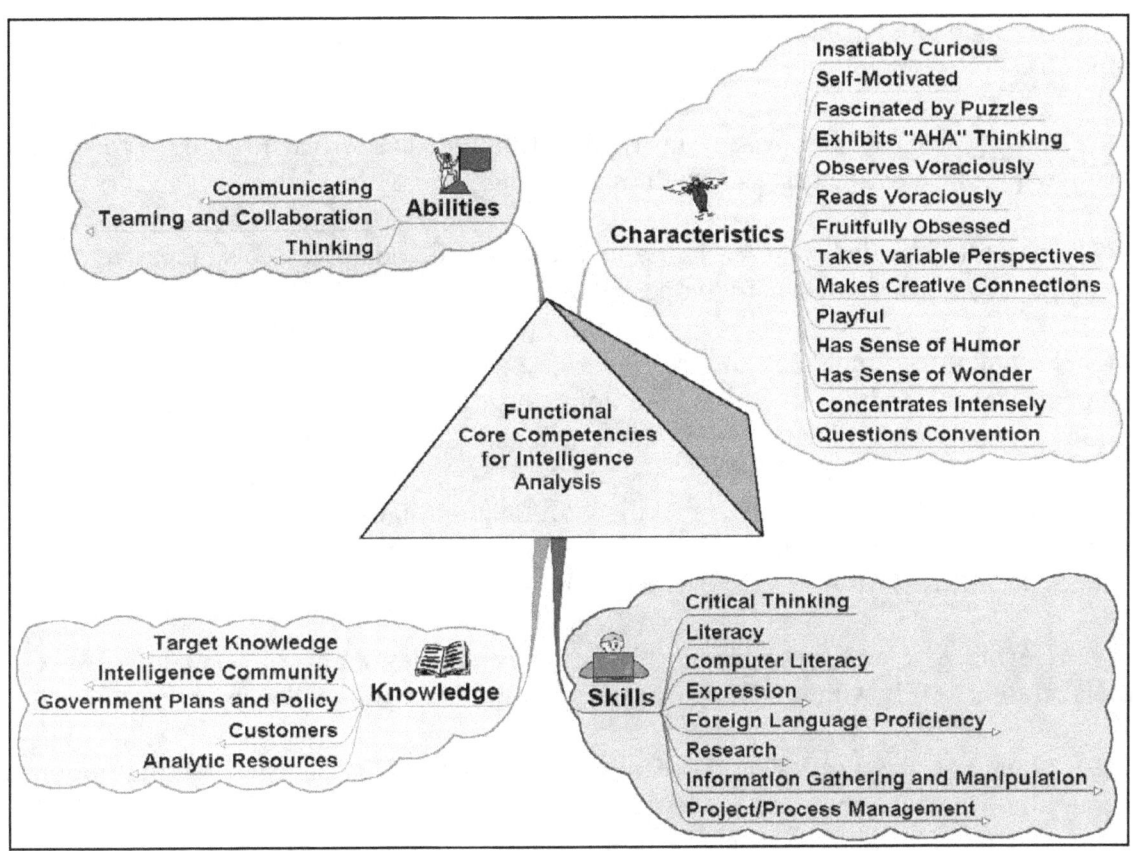

Figure F-1. Functional core competencies for intelligence analysis

F-4. Training

a. In 2016-2028, Army training design will have to accommodate what the educational capability of U.S. manpower pool provides and where necessary provide training that closes any gap between what is available and what the Army needs.

b. The Army IC challenge is to think beyond traditional business practices and to identify and adopt the methods and technological advances needed to provide the right knowledge, training, and education to Soldiers when and where needed to make a qualitative change in performance.

c. Institutional Army analyst and collector training will continue to be critical to the success of Army intelligence operations. The Army must develop innovative training techniques to integrate intuition and reasoning, heighten self-awareness, and foster adaptive decisionmaking under stress, urgency, and uncertainty. Possible efforts to improve training include the following:

(1) Commit to vigorous and constant learning with available analytic tools: model building, games, computer simulations, dialectic reasoning, and hypothesis testing.

(2) Augment traditional methods of instruction with interactive and immersive methods using personal computers, artificial intelligence, virtual reality, and simulations in a seamless

teaching environment; balance the benefits and risks associated with loss of social interaction or "campus life."

(3) Incorporate "learner based" instruction (multimedia, virtual learning, and eventually immersive) provided by the best and brightest instructors.

(4) Integrate intuition with reasoning and foster rapid, adaptive decisionmaking under the stress and uncertainty of full-spectrum operations.

(5) Conduct research study to determine the optimum days per week for analyst training looking at various training methods, environments, and cognitive development. Ask the question: Is the Army willing to commit the time it takes to train an entry level analyst?

(6) Challenge Soldier's analytical skills with tough problems that have no school solution. Use stress analysis and questioning, not just rote and group think. Encourage prudent risk taking (how does the Army shift from a risk adverse culture?).

(7) Devote time and space for questioning existing views and for objective research and analysis on future OE's within U.S. Army Intelligence Center of Excellence.

(8) Increase the use of Red Teaming methodology in analyst training to enhance vulnerability awareness and support the wide use of informed Red Teams in exercises and war games to enhance warfighter learning.

(9) Balance interpersonal and communication training with technical training.

(10) Provide a realistic simulated environment, and realistic simulation programs, that replicate the salient aspects of the OE to ensure Soldiers train as they fight.

(11) Training design must focus on developing analytical capabilities and not focus on rote memory learning.

(12) Training design must address train the trainer requirements to meet security force assistance and Homeland operations (state, local, tribal) mission's demands.

d. Cultural knowledge. Measures to overcome mirror imaging and educate MI Soldiers and leaders on cultural differences, geography, patterns of thought, and mind sets include the following.

(1) Geography. Issue computer software programs (such as, GeoQuest) to expand basic geographical knowledge of junior analysts. Provide incentives and engaging competitions to foster learning.

(2) Cultural awareness training for enlisted and officers to examine Soldiers' biases, attitudes, expectations, needs, and behavior. Make the training part of the teambuilding focus in professional military education.

(3) Standardized in-country training for intelligence analysts to expose them to various cultures. Work with country teams to rotate analysts for culture and language experience.

(4) Review the visualizations and displays of COP when conducting multinational operations. When the Army and its allies view the same picture, they may not see exactly what the Army sees and vice versa.

(5) Patterns of thought analysis, partnered with capabilities assessment, must begin with thorough understanding of the target culture and mind set.

(6) Encourage analysts to listen to the conversations of target audiences on the Internet in chat rooms, blogs, MySpace, YouTube, terrorist Web sites, videos, movies, and television channels.

(7) Cultural insight is found in humor, cartoons, literature, poetry, and children's stories. Incorporate these sources into analytical training. These may not seem likely sources of military intelligence, but they should be if we are interested in understanding and influencing various countries, cultures, or groups.

e. Irregular warfare training: The Army must develop irregular warfare and specific joint intelligence functional training that focuses on applying core intelligence tradecraft skills to regional problems and scenarios in each combatant command's AOR. The Army must develop a list of recommended irregular warfare related elective courses and training for intelligence personnel across echelons to improve knowledge of special capabilities. The special capabilities include counterterrorism network analysis, threat finance, IO, cyber warfare, use of hostile force-tagging, tracking, locating technologies, unattended sensors, ground SIGINT teams for target development, and close in targeting, biometrics, SSE, and DOMEX.

f. Intelligence partner training, The Army must partner in its intelligence training effort and build teaming relationships with colleges and university programs, which offer intelligence associated certificate and degree programs. These programs can parallel the professional military education levels. Several U.S. nongovernmental institutions offer undergraduate and graduate degrees in intelligence research and analysis, a sample of the programs are cited below in some detail. Other institutions include Fairmount University, Notre Dame College (Cleveland), Tennessee State University, Henley-Putnam University (online), James Madison University, Point Park University, University of Mississippi, and University of Texas at El Paso.

(1) Mercyhurst College, Pennsylvania. This school offers an undergraduate degree in intelligence studies. The goal of this program is to produce a graduate qualified for an entry-level position who has reading competency in a foreign language; a broad understanding of world and American history; a knowledge of comparative governments and political philosophies; the ability to produce written and oral reports and assessments based on research, correlation, and analysis; a familiarity with computer operations and database management; and a general understanding of statistical techniques. It also offers a Master of Science in Applied Intelligence. The applied intelligence graduate program provides students with the educational

foundation necessary to succeed as intelligence analysts and leaders of analytical teams at Federal and state agencies or within the law enforcement and business communities.

(2) Johns Hopkins University. This university offers a Master of Science in Intelligence Analysis degree. This degree program is specifically designed to serve students from various intelligence agencies—Federal, military, contractor, and law enforcement—to facilitate new relationships and transport layers, and breakdown traditional barriers to communication within the greater IC.

(3) The University of New Mexico expects to offer undergraduate through doctoral degrees in intelligence in the future, focusing on strategic intelligence.

(4) Embry-Riddle Aeronautical University offers a certificate program in intelligence and security through its campus and worldwide virtual program.

g. Foundry.

(1) Foundry provides a single hub for advanced skills training across the Active Army, Army National Guard, and the Army Reserve MI force. It also provides training to leaders supervising MI missions and Soldiers performing MI activities. Operational training is the process by which commands teach real world, mission required knowledge, skills, and abilities to Soldiers that result in improved mission capabilities and readiness. Foundry maintains and improves Army intelligence readiness through operational training that sustains highly perishable technical and low-density intelligence skills. Foundry supports individual and collective training by facilitating unit, functional partnerships, sustaining emerging technologies training, and providing sole source, all-source, SIGINT, MASINT, CI, HUMINT and GEOINT refresher training. It also supports reserve component integration efforts, and enables reachback multi security level transport layer connectivity from forward areas to intelligence training facilities. Foundry addresses the need for focused MI training not offered by TRADOC or the U.S. Army Forces Command.

(2) Foundry objectives include assisting tactical commanders in the technical training of their Soldier performing intelligence missions, helping the tactical force maintain contact with an adaptable adversary in an uncertain and complex operational environment, maintain a high state of readiness to enable intelligence driven operations for warfighting commanders, and training MI Soldiers to fight in an era of persistent conflict.

h. Language skills.

(1) The English language may not dominate the future Internet and other global communication mediums. This situation increases the Army's need for language training (such as, CI, HUMINT, SIGINT, OSINT, TECHINT collectors, and analysts). The Army needs a combination of new language training techniques and new language translation technologies to meet this challenge.

(2) Language training techniques. Though current Army language training provided by the Defense Language Institute is valuable, the institute's capabilities must improve in both techniques and technology. The Army requires enhanced language training capability in dialect specific terminology (ethnic and tribal), cyber terminology, and military and technical terminology.

i. Language translation techniques.

(1) Computer assisted. Also called computer-aided translation or machine-aided human translation, is a form of translation wherein a human translator creates a target text with the assistance of a computer program. The machine supports a human translator. Computer-assisted translation can include standard dictionary and grammar software. The term, however, normally refers to a range of specialized programs available to the translator, including translation-memory, terminology-management, concordance, and alignment programs.

(2) Machine translation is a subfield of computational linguistics that investigates the use of computer software to translate text or speech from one natural language to another. At its basic level, machine translation performs simple substitution of words in one natural language for words in another. Using these techniques, more complex translations may be accomplished. Further, this will help mitigate a projected shortfall of a human translator force in the future.

j. Institutional and unit training is required for intelligence support to civil support operations. These are operations conducted to address the consequences of natural or manmade disasters, accidents, and incidents within the U.S. and its territories. Army forces will engage in civil support operations when the size and scope of events exceed the capabilities of domestic civilian agencies. The Army National Guard often acts as a first responder on behalf of state authorities, when functioning under Title 32, U.S. Code authority, or while serving on state active duty. The candidate civil support training tasks include: application of the IPB process to civil support; intelligence support to incident awareness and assessment; intelligence support to civil law enforcement; intelligence support to disaster response; intelligence support to CBRNE consequence management; and intelligence support to pandemic disease support.

F-5. Materiel

a. Future intelligence capabilities must overcome complex terrain issues that diminish the effectiveness of current intelligence capabilities and increases the ability for future Army forces to detect enemy activity prior to engagement. Materiel acquisitions (such as, software, computers, vehicles, communications equipment, and others) must ensure maximum efficiency in maintainability, reliability, and operational effectiveness. Further, automation hardware acquisition must ensure maximum flexibility to accept new software or communication interfaces.

b. Automation capabilities. Future challenges in acquisition and application of automation support include requirements definition and the ambiguity of available future technology. MI Soldiers and leadership must embrace emerging technologies to ensure retention of the tactical and operational edge. Further, leaders must accept the risk that these technologies may not work as expected and accept failure as a means to move ahead. Some potential future automation examples and applications that may assist the intelligence warfighting function in dealing with increasing volume of information, dealing with degraded operations, and increased demand for analytic support (software and hardware) include the following:

(1) Quantum computing. The basic principle of quantum computation is that the quantum properties can be used to represent and structure data and that quantum mechanisms can be devised and built to perform operations with this data. Research in both theoretical and practical areas continues, and many national government and military funding agencies support quantum computing research to develop quantum computers for both civilian and national security purposes, such as for cryptanalysis.

(2) Cognitive radio. Cognitive radio is a paradigm for wireless communication in which either a transport layer or a wireless node changes its transmission or reception parameters to communicate efficiently avoiding interference with licensed or unlicensed users. This alteration of parameters is based on the active monitoring of several factors in the external and internal radio environments, such as radio frequency spectrum, user behavior, and transport layer state.

(3) Single-atom data storage, single molecule switching. The field of nanotechnology may lead to new kinds of devices and structures built from a few atoms or molecules. One such storage capability would enable nearly 30,000 feature length movies or the entire contents of YouTube – millions of videos estimated to be more than 1,000 trillion bits of data – to fit in a device the size of an iPod®.

c. Precision. Increased involvement in unconventional warfare increases the requirement for precision. Precision strike demands precise knowledge of self and opponent (capabilities and presence), and environment. The increased knowledge requirements will place enormous demands on future Army forces and its ability to acquire, transform, and provide knowledge.

d. Cyberspace operations. Collaborative planning, cooperative employment of capabilities, and rapid future Army force teaming introduce a significantly higher level of complexity and sophistication. Commanders and their staffs will contend with a dramatic increase in the amount and complexity of information required to plan and conduct operations. The Army will need a transport layer that facilitates full data access at all classification levels to future Army forces from the individual Soldier through national level. Cyberspace operations depend on the transport layer which increases the Army's vulnerability to computer transport layer attack.

e. High resolution weather observation and forecasting. High resolution weather observing and forecasting capabilities will improve forecast accuracy and environmental situational awareness by providing persistent stare and analysis capabilities to support tactical operations. Continuous weather observation and forecast updates eliminate environmental ambiguity and enable true mission command capabilities.

F-6. Leadership and education

a. Army leaders need to develop cohesive units that are effective in the asymmetrical fast paced future OE and are able to support multiple deployments with decreased reset times. The Army must not overemphasize data, technology, and analysis at the expense of relationships, trust, respect, common sense, and the intuition that comes from multiple combat tours in multiple AOs. A balance must be struck in developing leader cognitive, behavioral, and social skills. The future OE demands a clear accurate set of leader development criteria for training, operational assignments, and self-development.

b. In the future, joint and multinational operations leader development and training should address creative problem solving, language skills, cultural awareness, and the economic systems of other nations, team building, public relations, cross culture trust and use of technology, consensus building, and technology utilization and management.

c. Development and training should emphasize that combined arms operations in the future OE is more than armor, infantry, and artillery. It also includes intelligence, signal, civil affairs, military police, engineers, and others functions not normally considered under combined arms.

d. Future Army forces require critical and creative thinkers, agile, and able to make decisions in OEs replete with uncertainty, complexity, and change.

e. Future Army forces require experts of design and the remaining components of the operations process, capable of framing and reframing problems and shifting rapidly from preplanned action to action.

f. Empowering subordinates to employ the full array of combined arms capabilities, including those from joint, interagency, intergovernmental, and multinational partners, allows junior leaders to make timely decisions and exploit fleeting opportunities.

g. The IC faces a challenge expanding leader development into Reserve components with limited time, which begs the following questions.

(1) Given the current and future expanding role in future mission, what are the requirements to ensure quality reserve leaders?

(2) How can the Army harness reserve leader's development from the civilian life and careers?

(3) Self-development is particularly important for Reserve components. How can the Army leverage current and future technology and nongovernmental schooling to support reserve requirements?

(4) How does the Army address the availability of training allocations for reserve personnel?

(5) How does the army maintain the Reserve component's ability to support across operational commands to meet mission requirements?

d. Homeland security and civil support: Many authorizations and restrictions determine the use of U.S. military intelligence assets on U.S. soil. In homeland defense and civil support operations, commanders and their intelligence staffs must understand these often complex laws, rules, and regulations. Intelligence leadership and education programs must include such instruction as the differences between operations under Title 10 (active duty) versus Title 32 (National Guard). These programs must also emphasize close coordination with legal advisors, adherence to intelligence oversight policy and regulations, and coordination with domestic civilian organizations in such circumstances.

e. Professionalizing the ARSOF intelligence operator. The ARSOF intelligence structure has a two-fold mission to support both direct and indirect activities, particularly as they relate to irregular warfare. This requires planners, collection managers, collectors, and analysts capable of going beyond the six primary core military intelligence tasks (protection, situation development, target development, indications and warning, intelligence, and battle damage assessment). ARSOF intelligence operators, must not only be masters of F3EAD, but must also be well versed on the psychological, cultural, political, and human dimension of warfare. The ability to provide the commander information and intelligence to influence credibly relevant populations and nongovernmental centers of power is essential to ARSOF future successes.

F-7. Personnel

a. The Army should apply its limited resources towards revolutionary changes in accession, training, and retaining quality intelligence Soldiers and obtaining cutting edge software. Future Army forces must understand and utilize the strengths and mitigate the challenges of the three different generations that will make up the Army during the period 2016-2028 (see figure F-2.)

b. Future Army forces will need to pursue a broader approach to the recruitment and training of intelligence personnel. There is no single course of action the Army can pursue to assure a quality analytic workforce. Instead, it will have to execute multiple actions to address the problem. Acquisition of quality analysts will require characteristic assessment instruments, use of advanced civilian education, innovative military instruction, and selected recruitment of trained intelligence analysts from outside of the U.S. military. Army intelligence warfighting function recruiting must address the following:

(1) Develop cognitive profiles to recruit and assess intelligence analysts and leaders and eliminate those unlikely to succeed.

(2) Use cognitive assessment tools to measure ability and proclivity to reason using analogies and precedents.

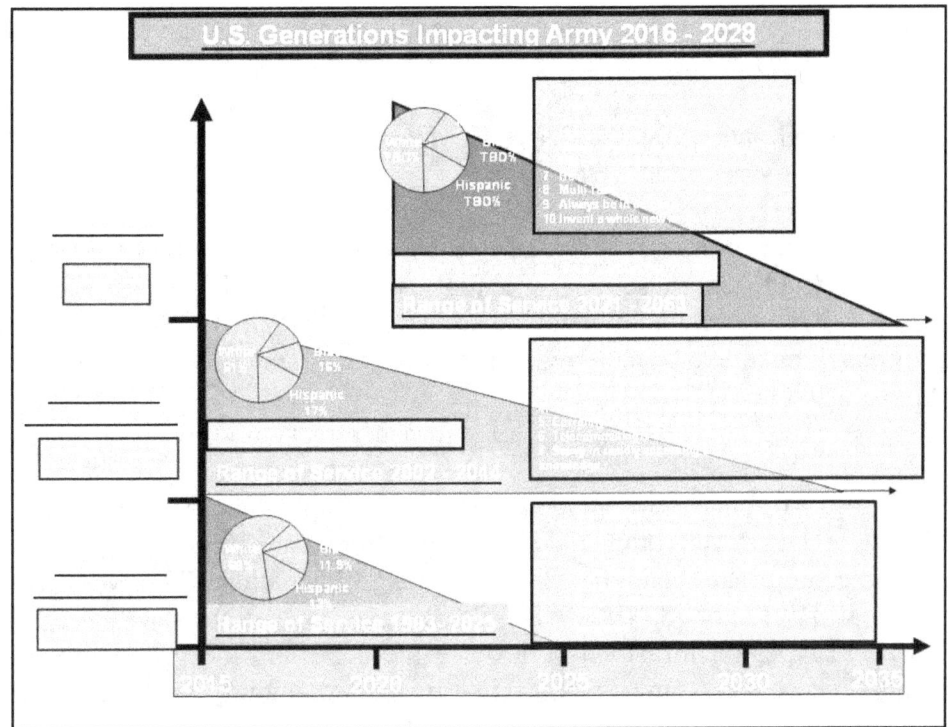

Figure F-2. U.S. generations affecting the Army in 2016-2028

(3) Recruit first and second generation interpreters and translators current in the languages and in modern slang and colloquialisms. Future Army forces need experts who understand history, including recent events. These Soldiers could operate in an unclassified and collateral environment (secret clearance). The Army must develop successful, rewarding career track to retain these specialists.

(4) Recruit or train specialists in semiotics (the science of symbols), which includes symbols, signs, gestures, and intonations.

(5) Recruit the right people to serve as analysts, not just the right number of people. The Army is in direct competition with national agencies, other services, academia, and industry for the best minds in America. We must publicly present Army intelligence as an attractive career option.

c. Retention and promotion. The Army must address the following in retention and promotion practices:

(1) Establish quick, non-retributive lateral transfers for those that cannot achieve required cognitive analytical standards.

(2) Eliminate "up or out" personnel policy if the Soldier is a great analyst but poor leader.

(3) Assign, promote, and reward successful instructors to ensure they remain motivated and competitive with peers.

(4) Continuous instructor evaluation to laterally move (no repercussions) substandard instructors.

(5) Allow enlisted and warrant officer specialization in specific adversaries or a specific AO.

d. In the effort to recruit the right personnel and to eliminate those unlikely to succeed, the Army must be careful to avoid serious potential pitfalls. The IC needs a broad range of personality type indicators and individuals who think and learn differently. Selection and screening programs must avoid the creation of an Army intelligence corps that may be susceptible to group think.

F-8. Facilities
The Army will need to pursue an upgrade of existing facilities and establish facilities to take advantage of state of the art computing and instructional hardware and software advances. It will need to modernize or procure facilities that provide infrastructure (hardware, software, and communication) such as, the Stryker BCT intelligence operations facility at Fort Lewis, Washington. These types of infrastructure provide the necessary tools to enable deployed and reset Army intelligence units to maintain intelligence continuity and support to mission command.

F-9. Homeland defense and civil support

a. The U.S. Army must plan for and provide intelligence support to commanders and civil authorities in defense of the homeland. This requires development of new capabilities for direction, management, and interoperability with Federal, state, tribal, and local entities when conducting intelligence operations in support of the homeland. These requirements effect all phases of intelligence operations (such as, collection, processing, analysis, and dissemination).

b. At a minimum the new measures must address civil to military and vice versa understanding of intelligence-specific definitions (such as, tactical, strategic intelligence, fusion, and others), intelligence sharing criteria, analytical standards, classification standards, communications standards, and regulatory and legal standards.

c. The *DOD Homeland Defense and Civil Support Joint Operating Concept* presents a strategic concept of an active, layered defense, which divides the world into three regions. Intelligence operations to support homeland defense must be proactive with focused efforts to support the regions specified below:

(1) Forward regions. The forward regions are foreign land areas, sovereign airspace, and sovereign waters outside the U.S.

(2) Approaches. The approaches are a conceptual region extending from the limits of the homeland to the forward regions based on situation-specific intelligence.

(3) Homeland. The homeland is a physical region that includes the land masses of the CONUS, Alaska, Hawaii; U.S. territories and possessions in the Caribbean Sea and Pacific Ocean; and the immediate surrounding sovereign waters and airspace.

d. USARNORTH.

(1) The principal ASCC for homeland defense is USARNORTH. USARNORTH operates in a changing and uncertain security environment. A range of threats, in all domains, represents an immediate and future challenge for the command. Whereas the enemies of yesterday were relatively predictable, homogeneous, hierarchical, and resistant to change, current adversaries include those who are unpredictable, diverse, thoroughly networked, and dynamic. These adversaries benefit from technologies and materials readily accessible in world markets, including disruptive systems and the ingredients required to fabricate WMD. USARNORTH shares the fundamental responsibility of defending the U.S. homeland as well as the broader USARNORTH AOR from external threats.

(2) Homeland defense is USARNORTH's top priority in support of securing the U.S. from direct attack through an active defense. In addition to its primary role, USARNORTH must also be prepared to provide DSCA and support to U.S. civil authorities (Federal, state, local, and tribal) by responding to natural and manmade disasters. Natural disasters, such as hurricanes, earthquakes, or pandemics, can exceed the capabilities of civilian responders, and thus require significant allocation of military resources to help mitigate their effects and to support relief and recovery efforts. Likewise, a terrorist attack, particularly one involving WMD, can cause catastrophic losses requiring substantial civil support and DSCA.

e. Operations outside the U.S.: In the forward regions and approaches, deployed intelligence elements BCT through ASCC are tasked to provide homeland defense and civil support intelligence through normal PIR, CCIR, and intelligence, surveillance, and reconnaissance synchronization processes. Reporting and dissemination would be dictated by METT-TC and existing operational directives.

f. Operations inside the U.S.: Army intelligence operations in the homeland will be primarily executed by USNORTHCOM and INSCOM intelligence organizations and staffs. All U.S. nondeployed intelligence capabilities (BCT to theater Army) are available for homeland defense and civil support missions based on METT-TC and legal consideration.[9] At a minimum, all U.S. based intelligence organizations active, National Guard, and reserve should expect to provide their appropriate commander(s) with intelligence support to base and facility security operations, personnel security operations, and indications and warning for their unit's specific AOR.

g. Many laws and policies determine the use of U.S. military intelligence assets on U.S. soil. In homeland defense and civil support operations, commanders and their intelligence staffs must understand these often complex laws, rules, and regulations. These policies generally restrict domestic intelligence activities to foreign and counter intelligence.[10] Intelligence leadership and education programs must include such instruction as the differences between operations under Title 10 (active duty) versus Title 32 (National Guard). These programs must also emphasize close coordination with legal advisors, adherence to intelligence oversight policy and regulations, and coordination with domestic civilian organizations in such circumstances.

F-10. Intelligence sharing

Intelligence sharing is primarily the result of establishing a Web-based collaborative environment. Collaboration includes the sharing of knowledge, expertise, and information, normally online. Collaboration may take many forms. Collaborative tools include computer based tools that help individuals work together and share information. These tools allow for virtual online meetings and data sharing. Sharing allows analysts, other intelligence personnel, and other subject matter experts to freely exchange information and intelligence to assist in answering their commander's requirements. The intelligence staff must identify the most effective methods to share intelligence with all required users (joint, interagency, intergovernmental, and multinational). Sharing applies specifically to multinational partners, who are unable to access U.S. information systems or data files. Some users may require hardcopy printouts of new or updated intelligence; some may simply need to access the unit intelligence Web page; and some may simply require access to specific unit databases.

Glossary

Section I
Abbreviations

AO	area of operations
AOR	area of responsibility
ARCIC	Army Capabilities Integration Center
ARSOF	Army special operations forces
ASCC	Army service component command
BCT	brigade combat team
CBRNE	chemical, biological, radiological, nuclear, and high-yield explosives
CCIR	commanders critical information requirements
CI	counterintelligence
CNO	computer network operations
COA	course(s) of action
CoIST	company intelligence support teams
CONUS	continental U.S.
COP	common operational picture
DA	Department of the Army
DOD	Department of Defense
DOMEX	document and media exploitation
DOTMLPF	doctrine, organization, training, materiel, leadership and education, personnel and facilities
DSCA	defense support of civil authorities
ES	electronic warfare support
F3EAD	find, fix, finish, exploit, analyze, and disseminate
FFIR	friendly force information requirements
FM	field manual
GCC	geographic combatant commander
GEOINT	geospatial intelligence
HQ	headquarters
HUMINT	human intelligence
IC	intelligence community
INSCOM	Intelligence and Security Command
IO	information operations
IPB	intelligence preparation of the battlefield
JFLCC	joint force land component commander
JP	joint publication
JSOTF	joint special operations task force
MASINT	measurement and signature intelligence
METT-TC	mission, enemy, terrain and weather, troops and support available, time available, and civil considerations
MI	military intelligence
MSO	military source operation

OCONUS	outside the continental U.S.
OE	operational environment
OIF	Operation Iraqi Freedom
OSINT	open-source intelligence
Pam	pamphlet
PIR	primary intelligence requirement
PMESII-PT	political, military, economic, social, infrastructure, and information physical environment and time
SIGINT	signals intelligence
SOF	special operations forces
SSE	sensitive site exploitation
TECHINT	technical intelligence
TRADOC	Training and Doctrine Command
TSOC	theater special operations command
UAS	unmanned aircraft system
U.S.	United States
USARNORTH	U.S. Army North
USASOC	U.S. Army Special Operations Command
USNORTHCOM	U.S. Northern Command
WMD	weapons of mass destruction

Section II
Terms

air defense
All defensive measures designed to destroy attacking enemy aircraft or missiles in the Earth's envelope of atmosphere, or to nullify or reduce the effectiveness of such attack.

all-source intelligence
Intelligence products and/or organizations and activities that incorporate all sources of information, most frequently including human resources intelligence, imagery intelligence, measurement and signature intelligence, signals intelligence, and open-source data in the production of finished intelligence. In intelligence collection, a phrase that indicates that in the satisfaction of intelligence requirements, all collection, processing, exploitation, and reporting systems and resources are identified for possible use and those most capable are tasked. Intelligence that is produced through the analysis of all available information obtained through intelligence, surveillance, and reconnaissance operations (FM 34-1).

area of interest
That area of concern to the commander, including the area of influence, areas adjacent thereto, and extending into enemy territory to the objectives of current or planned operations. This area also includes areas occupied by enemy forces that could jeopardize the accomplishment of the mission (FM 3-0).

area of operations
An operational area defined by the joint force commander for land and maritime forces. Areas of operation do not typically encompass the entire operational area of the joint force commander, but should be large enough for component commanders to accomplish their missions and protect their forces (FM 3-0).

area of responsibility
The geographical area associated with a combatant command within which a combatant commander has authority to plan and conduct operations.

base support installation
A DOD service or agency installation with the U.S., its territories, or possessions tasked to serve as a base for military forces engaged in either homeland defense or civil support operations (JP 3-28).

civil support
DOD support to U.S. civil authorities for domestic emergencies, and for designated law enforcement and other activities (JP 3-28).

collection
In intelligence usage, the acquisition of information and the provision of this information to processing elements.

collection management
In intelligence usage, the process of converting intelligence requirements into collection requirements, establishing priorities, tasking or coordinating with appropriate collection sources or agencies, monitoring results, and retasking, as required (JP 2-0).

combat information
Unevaluated data, gathered by or provided directly to the tactical commander which, due to its highly perishable nature or the criticality of the situation, cannot be processed into tactical intelligence in time to satisfy the user's tactical intelligence requirements.

common operational picture
A single display of relevant information within a commander's area of interest tailored to the user's requirements and based on common data and information shared by more than one command (JP 3-0).

counterintelligence
Information gathered and activities conducted to protect against espionage, other intelligence activities, sabotage, or assassinations conducted by or on behalf of foreign governments or elements thereof, foreign organizations, or foreign persons, or international terrorist activities (JP 2-0).

cyberspace
A global domain within the information environment consisting of the interdependent network of information technology infrastructures, including the Internet, telecommunications networks, computer systems, and embedded processors and controllers (JP 1-02).

decentralized operations
The delegation of authority and capabilities to design, plan, prepare, execute, and adapt military action within the intended purpose of higher HQ' mission.

effect
The physical or behavioral state of a system that results from an action, a set of actions, or another effect. The result, outcome, or consequence of an action. A change to a condition, behavior, or degree of freedom (JP 3-0).

electronic warfare
Military action involving the use of electromagnetic and directed energy to control the electromagnetic spectrum or to attack the enemy. Electronic warfare consists of three divisions: electronic attack, electronic protection, and electronic warfare support.

full-spectrum operations
The range of operations Army forces conduct in war and military operations other than war.

geospatial intelligence
The exploitation and analysis of imagery and geospatial information to describe, assess, and visually depict physical features and geographically referenced activities on the Earth. Consists of imagery, imagery intelligence, and geospatial information (JP 2-03).

homeland
The physical region that includes the CONUS, Alaska, Hawaii, and U.S. territories and possessions, and surrounding territorial waters and airspace (JP 3-28).

homeland defense
The protection of U.S. sovereignty, territory, domestic population, and critical infrastructure against external threats and aggression or other threats as directed by the President (JP 3-27).

homeland security
Homeland security, as defined in the National Strategy for Homeland Security, is a concerted national effort to prevent terrorist attacks within the U.S., reduce America's vulnerability to terrorism, and minimize the damage and recover from attacks that do occur (JP 3-28).

human intelligence
A category of intelligence derived from information collected and provided by human sources (JP 2-0).

imagery intelligence
The technical, geographic, and intelligence information derived through the interpretation or analysis of imagery and collateral materials (JP 2-0).

indications and warning
Those intelligence activities intended to detect and report time sensitive intelligence information on foreign developments that could involve a threat to the U.S. or allied and/or coalition military, political, or economic interests or to U.S. citizens abroad. Includes forewarning of hostile actions or intentions against the U.S., its activities, overseas forces, or allied and/or coalition nations (JP 2-0).

information
Facts, data, or instructions in any medium or form. The meaning that a human assigns to data by means of the known conventions used in their representation (JP 3-13.1).

inform and influence activities
The integrated employment of the core capabilities of electronic warfare, computer transport layer operations, psychological operations, military deception, and operations security, in concert with specified supporting and related capabilities, to influence, disrupt, corrupt or usurp adversarial human and automated decisionmaking while protecting our own.

information requirements
Those items of information regarding the enemy and his environment which need to be collected and processed to meet the intelligence requirements of a commander. All information necessary to address the factors of METT-TC.

information superiority
That degree of dominance in the information domain which permits the conduct of operations without effective opposition. The operational advantage derived from the ability to collect, process, and disseminate an uninterrupted flow of information while exploiting or denying an adversary's ability to do the same (FM 3-0).

intelligence
The product resulting from the collection, processing, integration, analysis, evaluation, and interpretation of available information concerning foreign countries or areas. Information and knowledge about an adversary obtained through observation, investigation, analysis, or understanding.

intelligence community
All departments or agencies of a government that are concerned with intelligence activity, either in an oversight, managerial, support, or participatory role (JP 2-01.2).

intelligence, surveillance, and reconnaissance
An activity that synchronizes and integrates the planning and operation of sensors, assets, and processing, exploitation, and dissemination systems in direct support of current and future operations. This is an integrated intelligence and operations function (JP 2-01).

joint force commander
A general term applied to a combatant commander, subunified commander, or joint task force commander authorized to exercise combatant command (command authority) or operational control over a joint force (JP 1).

joint task force
A joint force that is constituted and so designated by the Secretary of Defense, a combatant commander, a subunified commander, or an existing joint task force commander (JP 1).

knowledge
In the context of the cognitive hierarchy, information analyzed to provide meaning and value or evaluated as to implications for the operation (FM 6-0).

measurement and signature intelligence
Scientific and technical intelligence obtained by quantitative and qualitative analysis of data (metric, angle, spatial, wavelength, time dependence, modulation, plasma, and hydromagnetic) derived from specific technical sensors for the purpose of identifying any distinctive features associated with the target, source, emitter, or sender measurement of the same. The detected feature may be either reflected or emitted (FM 34-1).

near real time
Pertaining to the timeliness of data or information which has been delayed by the time required for electronic communication and automatic data processing. This implies that there are no significant delays.

nonlethal
Neutralizing or incapacitating a target without causing permanent injury, death, or gross physical destruction.

nongovernmental organization
Transnational organizations of private citizens that maintain a consultative status with the Economic and Social Council of the United Nations. Nongovernmental organizations may be professional associations, foundations, multinational businesses, or simply groups with a common interest in humanitarian assistance activities (development and relief) (FM 3-07).

open source intelligence
Information of potential intelligence value that is available to the general public (JP 2-0).

operational environment
A composite of the conditions, circumstances, and influences that affect the employment of capabilities and bear on the decisions of the commander (JP 3-0).

persistent surveillance
The synchronization and integration of available transport layered sensors and analysts across warfighting functions and operational environments, to provide commanders with combat information, actionable intelligence and situational understanding. A collection strategy that

emphasizes the ability of some collection systems to linger on demand in an area to detect, locate, characterize, identify, track, target, and possibly provide battle damage assessment and retargeting in near or real-time (JP 1-02). Joint and multinational operations—inclusive of normal and routine military activities—and various interagency activities are performed to dissuade or deter potential adversaries and to assure or solidify relationships with friends and allies (JP 3-0).

police intelligence operations
A military police function that supports, enhances, and contributes to the commander's force protection program, common operational picture, and situational understanding. Ensures that information collected during the conduct of other military police functions is provided as input to the intelligence collection effort and turned into action or reports (FM 7-15).

reach
A process by which military forces proactively and rapidly access information, receive support, and conduct direct collaboration and information sharing with other units and agencies both deployed in theater and outside the theater unconstrained by geographic proximity, echelon, or command.

real-time
Pertaining to the timeliness of data or information which has been delayed only by the time required for electronic communication. This implies that there are no noticeable delays.

reconnaissance
A mission undertaken to obtain, by visual observation or other detection methods, information about the activities and resources of an enemy or potential enemy, or to secure data concerning the meteorological, hydrographic, or geographic characteristics of a particular area (JP 2-0).

request for information
Any specific time-sensitive ad hoc requirement for intelligence information or products to support an ongoing crisis or operation not necessarily related to standing requirements or scheduled intelligence production. A request for information can be initiated to respond to operational requirements and will be validated in accordance with the combatant command's procedures (JP 2-0).

surveillance
The systematic observation of aerospace, surface or subsurface areas, places, persons, or things by visual, aural, electronic, photographic, or other means (FM 34-1).

synchronization
The arrangement of military actions in time, space, and purpose to produce maximum relative combat power at a decisive place and time. In the intelligence context, application of intelligence sources and methods in concert with the operational plan (FM 34-2).

technical intelligence
Intelligence derived from exploitation of foreign material, produced for strategic, operational, and tactical level commanders. Begins when an individual service member finds something new on the battlefield and takes proper steps to report it. The item is then exploited at succeedingly higher levels until a countermeasure is produced to neutralize the adversary's technological advantage.

unmanned aircraft
An aircraft or balloon that does not carry a human operator and is capable of flight under remote control or autonomous programming (JP 3-03).

unmanned aircraft system
That system whose components include the necessary equipment, network, and personnel to control an unmanned aircraft (JP 3-03).

Section III
Special Terms

co-creation of context
A continuous process in which commanders direct intelligence priorities to drive operations, and the intelligence that these operations produce causes commanders to refine operations based on an improved understanding of the situation.

combined arms
The combination of the elements of combat power with the integration and sequencing of all actions, activities, and programs necessary to seize, retain, and exploit the initiative in the context of full-spectrum operations.

combined arms maneuver
The application of the elements of combat power in a complementary and reinforcing manner to achieve physical, temporal, or psychological advantages over the enemy, preserve freedom of action, and exploit success.

computational linguistics
An interdisciplinary field dealing with the statistical and/or rule-based modeling of natural language from a computational perspective. This modeling is not limited to any particular field of linguistics.

concordance
An alphabetical list of the principal words used in a book or body of work, with their immediate contexts.

concordancer
A computer program that automatically constructs a concordance. The output of a concordancer may serve as input to a translation memory system for computer-assisted translation, or as an early step in machine translation.

mission command
The exercise of authority and direction by commanders, supported by their staffs, using the art of command and the science of control to integrate warfighting functions in the conduct of full-spectrum operations. Mission command uses mission orders to ensure disciplined initiative within the commander's intent, enabling agile and adaptive commanders, leaders, and organizations.

network
A single, secure, standards-based, versatile infrastructure linked by networked, redundant transport systems, sensors, warfighting and business applications, and services that provide Soldiers and civilians timely and accurate information in any environment, to manage the Army enterprise and enable full-spectrum operations with joint, allied, and interagency partners.

operating decentralized
A manner of conducting military operations which enables subordinates to act aggressively and independently with disciplined initiative to develop the situation; seize, retain, and exploit the initiative; and cope with uncertainty to accomplish the mission within the commander's intent.

operational adaptability
A quality that Army leaders and forces exhibit based on critical thinking, comfort with ambiguity and decentralization, a willingness to accept prudent risk, and ability to make rapid adjustments based on a continuous assessment of the situation.

translation memory
A database that stores so-called segments, which can be sentences or sentence-like units (headings, titles, or elements in a list), that have been previously translated. A translation-memory system stores the words, phrases, and paragraphs that have already been translated and aid human translators.

wide area security
The application of the elements of combat power in coordination with other military and civilian capabilities to deny the enemy positions of advantage; protect forces, populations, infrastructure, and activities; and consolidate tactical and operational gains to set conditions for achieving strategic and policy goals.

Endnotes

[1] *Fixing Intel A Blueprint for Making Intelligence Relevant in Afghanistan,* MG Michael T. Flynn, USA, CPT Matt Pottinger, USMC, and Paul D. Batchelor, Defense Intelligence Agency, Joint Center for Operational Analysis Journal, vol XI, issue 3, fall 2009.

[2] FM 3-0 glossary 8.

[3] Summary, Commander's Appreciation and Campaign Design.

[4] Schultz, Jr., R. H & Godson, R. *Intelligence Dominance A Better Way Forward in Iraq.* 3.

[5] FM 3-0, glossary 8.

[6] Schultz, Jr., R. H & Godson, R. *Intelligence Dominance A Better Way Forward in Iraq.* 3.

[7] Ibid. 4-4.

[8] Swenson, Russell, G. (May 2003). Bringing Intelligence About: Practitioners Reflect on Best Practices. Joint Military Intelligence College, Washington DC, Center for Strategic Intelligence Research.

[9] DOD 5240.1-R. Procedures governing the activities of DOD intelligence components that affect United States persons.

[10] EO 12333, United States Intelligence Activities, DODD 5240.1. DoD Intelligence Activities, DOD 5240.1-R, Procedures governing the activities of DOD intelligence components that affect United States persons, and DODD 5525.5, DOD Cooperation with Civilian Law Enforcement Officials.

www.ingramcontent.com/pod-product-compliance
Lightning Source LLC
Chambersburg PA
CBHW081406280526
45788CB00009B/3005